SECULAR SACRAMENTS

FINDING GRACE IN THE WORLD AND SIN IN
THE CHURCH

DUSTIN MESSER

Center for Cultural Leadership
P. O. Box 100
Coulterville, California 95311
831-420-7230
www.christianculture.com

The Center for Cultural Leadership is a non-profit Christian educational foundation devoted to influencing Christians for effective cultural leadership — in church, the arts, education, business, technology, science, and other realms of contemporary culture.

❀ Created with Vellum

CONTENTS

ACKNOWLEDGMENTS

There are several people and organization who must be thanked for making this project possible. First, thank you to the various outlets that first published these essays, including Christianity Today, The Gospel Coalition, The Colson Center, Dordt College's Center for the Advancement of Christian Education, The Ethics and Religious Liberty Commission, Mere Orthodoxy, Mockingbird, The Institute for Faith, Work, and Economics, Southern Seminary, The Theopolis Institute, truthXchange, Kuyperian Commentary, and the Circe Institute. Thanks to P. Andrew Sandlin for the generous invitation to write this book – it's only one of many graces Andrew has shown me. The parts of the book that are more theological in tone couldn't have been written apart from the tutelage of Brian Payne – my pastor, professor, mentor, and friend. The parts of the book that deal more directly with cultural apologetics are heavily influenced by Mark Ryan, who introduced me to the connective tissue of reality, showing me that to talk about anything is to talk about everything. Thanks also to my brother in arms, Uri Brito, who was the first person to give me an opportunity to write for a popular audience. For those with eyes to see, Uri's fingerprints are all over this book.

Much of the content herein began as classroom discussions at Legacy Christian Academy, Frisco, TX, where I teach in the high school Bible department. Thanks to Bill McGee, Kevin Mosley, Daniel Townsley, Ronnie Littleton, Chris Harmon, and particularly Adam Housley, who first brought me to Legacy. The clergy and laity at both Christ Church Carrollton and All Saints Dallas have likewise been unbelievably supportive as I've thought through the themes in these essays along with them. To my parents, Jeff and Donna Messer, for their unwavering love and guidance – thank you. Thanks also to my in-laws, Greg and Debbie Meador, for their support and care. Lastly, but most importantly, I'd like to thank Whitney Messer, my wife, friend, editor, and teacher. Thank you, Whitney, for being the best part of me – this book is dedicated to you.

PREFACE

Over 25 years ago, when I was about the age Dustin Messer is now, a noted elderly theologian paid me an unusual compliment I'll never forget: "Andrew, you don't practice pure theology." While I'm generally reluctant to publicize (the few) compliments I've gotten over the years, I'm airing this one precisely because of its pertinence to Dustin's book. The aged theologian did not mean by "pure" theology, theology purged from error. He meant theology sequestered from contemporary culture. We sometimes encounter the expression "ivory-tower theology," and there can be no doubt that too much theology today is designed to be read by and practiced exclusively within the church or, even worse, the academy.

This truncation is particularly characteristic of conservative theology. It is liberal theology that is culturally engaged. Unfortunately, theological liberalism long ago surrendered the pole of biblical authority and Christian orthodoxy, so its cultural engagement is relativist. Conservative theology is culturally irrelevant, and liberal theology is culturally rudderless. The proper alternative is relevant theology whose rudder is the infallible word of God.

This is the theology Dustin Messer offers in this veritable kaleidoscope of entries. Only a theologian marinated in Reformational philosophy in the tradition of Abraham Kuyper, Herman Dooyeweerd, and Francis Schaeffer could write with such verve and authority on such a wide range of topics. The reason is easy to define, even if it is difficult to implement: Jesus is Lord of all of life; therefore, all of life is subject to reordering according to his word.

Dustin is truly a Christian Renaissance man, equally at home in the church, academy, and the culture; these entries reflect a truly evangelized mind (in the language of T. F. Torrance), that is, an intellect that has been fused with the comprehensive gospel of Jesus Christ. For this reason alone this book deserves to be read with the greatest attention.

P. Andrew Sandlin
Founder & President
Center for Cultural Leadership

INTRODUCTION

When the idea first came up of publishing a collection of my essays in one volume, I doubted the viability of the project. Nevertheless, I decided to look over my output from the past couple of years to see if a theme emerged that might give an anthology some coherence. I was pleasantly surprised to indeed see a unifying thread, namely, admitting the church's sin and recognizing the grace that's present in the world. In other words, these essays are my attempt to read culture theologically and understand the church culturally.

There are moments, even in our secular, de-mythologized West, where the transcendent shines through in unlikely places —films, pop-music, etc. If we're looking with eyes of faith, we can see grace in the world. The book's title is a double entendre, though. Not only are there pointers and signs of grace in the secular world, but if we look closely at the church, it's obvious that her sacramental life has too often become secularized. This book, then, seeks to celebrate the goodness in the world while confessing the sin that's in the church.

An example may help in setting the tone of the book. Not too long ago, I was interviewed on a Christian radio station. In the segment before I went on, the DJ said, "isn't it fair to say that the message of the Bile is, 'follow your heart?'"

Later that same day, I watched Pixar's *Coco*. If you've seen the movie, you know that Miguel wants to leave his family, people, and culture to remake himself solely based on his talent, passion, etc. "Following his heart" kills him—literally, he's damned. It's only when he submits himself to his tradition, looking outside of himself for identity, purpose, and meaning that he's able to find life—literally, he's resurrected.

It was beautiful, good, and true. At the end of that day, it occurred to me that it was Christians—not Disney—that preached expressive individualism to me. As Abraham Kuyper used to say, "The world is often better than we might expect, and the church worse." This book follows this rhythm of celebration and confession.

What this book does not offer, however, is a theory of cultural apologetics—though such a project would no doubt be worthwhile. Instead, it offers my attempt to *do* cultural apologetics, however imperfectly, as taught to me by people like Mark Ryan, Dick Keyes, William Edgar, Tim Keller, Os Guinness, Joe Boot, and Andrew Sandlin.

I was tempted to edit these essays with a more heavy hand —removing phrases like, "a few days ago," for instance—but in the end, I decided to largely let them stand as they first appeared in print or online, for better or worse. Each essay basically stands on its own and be read in any order. My prayer is that these essays will, in some small way, encourage you to more boldly and gracefully offer a reason for the hope that's within you.

1

THE PALEO-ORTHODOX DIET

In his book *In Defense of Food* Michael Pollan does just what the title suggests, he defends food. Pollan argues that the presupposition behind modern food science, or "nutritionism" as he calls it, is that humans don't need food, they need nutrients. To be sure, modern science is not yet unified on exactly what nutrients mankind might best thrive on, but they are convinced that the perfect diet is to be found not in a kitchen, but in a lab.

Says Pollan: "if you're a nutrition scientist you do the only thing you can do, given the tools at your disposal: break the thing down into its component parts and study those one by one, even if that means ignoring the subtle interactions and contexts and the fact that the whole may well be more than, or maybe just different from, the sum of its parts."

In other words, if you ask a scientist "what is an apple?" don't be surprised when he answers by describing the pieces he just examined under a microscope. He's answering the question with the skill set and worldview with which he was trained.

Contra such reductionist science, Pollan argues that an apple is an entity in and of itself. Its benefits can't be replicated simply by taking the exact dosage of Vitamins K, B-6, and E found in the fruit. No, in order to thrive, we need the apple, not simply its "nutrients."

If Pollan is right when he says that we need food (i.e. fruits, vegetables, meat, seeds, etc.) rather than simply nutrients (i.e. vitamins, minerals, chemicals, etc.), then the answer to the question "what should we eat?" won't be found in labs, but in kitchens. In the end, Pollan's book is as much cultural history as it is dietary advice. Nutritionism, it becomes clear, is simply the outworking of an arrogant modernity which equates knowledge with the scientific method. It is produced by a culture which views itself, as Wendell Berry might say, more machine than human.

In his book *The Death of Scripture and the Rise of Biblical Studies* Michael Legaspi tells the same story of modernity but with Scripture, rather than food, as the subject. If the books are read together, it becomes clear that the worldview which led us from the kitchen to the lab also led us from the church to the academy. Focusing on the ways in which Scripture was used and re-imagined in eighteenth-century Germany, Legaspi skillfully shows that the Enlightenment attempted to fit the Bible into the category of "text" rather than "Scripture."

Legaspi says it well, "Academic critics did not dispense with the authority of a Bible resonant with religion; they redeployed it. Yet they did so in a distinctive form that has run both parallel and perpendicular to church appropriations of the Bible." In other words, the same Bible was being studied in the academy as in the church, but the academy had vastly different goals, values, and presuppositions motivating its study.

Thus, Legaspi recounts the history of modern biblical interpretation as a move from "Scripture" (which is read in the church) to "text" (which is read in the academy). If one asks a biblical scholar "what does this text mean?" one shouldn't be surprised when he answers by simply parsing the set of words in front of him. He's answering the question with the skillset and worldview with which he was trained. Just as modern nutritionism views food as simply a collection of vitamins and calories, never considering the context of the whole food, never mind the whole meal, so too does the modern biblical scholar neglect the canonical context in which a given passage finds itself, as well as the context in which the text was meant to be read.

For those with eyes to see, Legaspi's use of the word "text" is reminiscent of Pollan's use of the word "nutrients." A text, like a nutrient, lies on the table in front of the critic, waiting to be broken into its parts and put under a microscope for scientific study. Scripture, on the other hand, is like food. It comes on its own terms, demanding to be eaten "as is." Scripture is more than, and different than, the sum of its parts.

For example, to "know" the story of the Good Samaritan in a textual sense simply involves issues of grammar, syntax, and cultural idiosyncrasies. To "know" the story in a Scriptural sense involves all those things, but also a willingness to view the needy around you as your neighbor. Said differently, to know a *text* exclusively involves one's cognitive faculties. Knowing *scripture*, however, might begin with the mind, but if it doesn't end in full-bodied obedience, it isn't truly known. This, I take it, is the point of James 1:23-25.

If the story being told by Pollan is that of nutritionism, then the story being told by Legaspi is what I'll call "textism." Because nutritionism and textism are both products of modernism, it will behoove those of us concerned with practicing an ancient, ecclesial, Paleo-faith to study the practices of those rejecting the dietary outworking's of modernism. Their journey to the kitchen, in many ways, will show us the road back to the church. For example, let's consider three of the questions Pollan recommends asking before buying food: Is this a "food?" Would my ancestors recognize it as a food? Is it local?

First, is this a "food?" As we've seen, when Pollan uses the word "food" he's trying to undermine modern nutritionism. He wouldn't want us to consider a pill which claims to have the same nutritional make-up as a squash equivalent with a squash. If you want the benefits of a squash, there is no pill, or for that matter cereal, which can equate the actual eating of a squash. Thus, when we go to the grocery store, we have to reckon with the actual creature in front of us, rather than viewing the object as a collection of mere nutrients.

When we open our Bibles, we have to ask "is this Scripture?" By answering in the affirmative, we will undermine the modernist attempt to neuter the Bible into a "text." A text is private; Scripture is public. Textism has produced a private reading of Scripture which, at best, will demand the reader take every "*spiritual*" thought captive to Christ. A Scriptural reading will call the reader to take every thought captive: from politics to business to family-life. There isn't a sphere in which the King, speaking through the Scriptures, does not demand obedience from the reader.

Likewise, a text is read rationalistically; Scripture is read theologically. A theological interpretation of Scripture is the natural consequence of recognizing the Scriptures as such. If the same Spirit who inspired Micah inspired John, then making intertextual, typological connection is not artificial, but natural, and indeed necessary! A text has one author; Scripture has two.

While the divine author is never in conflict with the human author, we should expect the divine authorial intent to be "thicker" than the human author's intent. Said differently, the same Author who started the story (in Genesis) had the climax (in the Gospels) and the ending (in Revelation) in mind all the way through. Thus, it is only natural that we recognize the substance (the thing typified) in the shadow (the type).

Second, would my ancestors recognize it as a food? Pollan points out that while your ancestors might mistake *Go-Gurt®* as yogurt, they certainly wouldn't recognize its gelatin or modified cornstarch as food. At some point, modern eating has departed from what traditional cultures would recognize as food. In the same way, Scripture demands to be read in a way congruent with the past. To be sure, Scripture always trumps any past interpretation of itself, but we would be fools to neglect the wisdom of our fathers. Thus, we can read, say, the account of Jesus' baptism with the Trinitarian creeds in the back of our minds. We do this not with a slavish obedience to "tradition," but with the humility and confidence which comes with being part of a church that transcends time and space.

Third, is it local? The modernist worldview has made the purchasing of food as abstract, impersonal, and unaccountable as possible. The orange we eat this morning was just as likely to have been picked in Mexico as Florida. The ways in which the farmer treats his employees, we're told, is not our business. However, when one buys locally, not only is the grower made accountable to the eater, but the eater is brought into a relationship with the farmer, the merchant, and indeed the land. In other words, to buy locally is to subject yourself to a community.

Scripture, likewise, must be read locally, in community. Texts are read individually, often at a desk, with a pen and dictionary in hand. Of course, it is perfectly appropriate to study the Scriptures on one's own; but that is not the natural way in which to read the Scriptures. The Scriptures were written to be heard, and rehearsed, in the context of a church. Thus, if one tries to exclusively read, say, the Psalms on one's own, the lament Psalms are either muted, or applied to fairly trivial matters. If read in community, these Psalms are read (or sung) with the experiences of others in mind. True, every individual person may not be suffering in a given congregation, but someone in the church is. And, when read communally the suffering person's burdens are borne by the whole community.

Additionally, when Scripture is read in community, the interpretation of each reader is accountable not only to the ancient church, but to the local church. The perspectives of various genders, ages, cultures, and ethnicities work as a safeguard for any one person's interpretation. Reading Scripture is a communal act in which each individual reader is brought into an accountable relationship with every other reader.

Michael Pollan feels compelled to defend food because he lives a midst a people whose obsession with nutrition has left them malnourished. They keep eating nutrients in what he calls "food like substances," but never pick up what our ancestors would recognize as food. Likewise, the result of textism is a people who don't know how to read the text of Scripture.

Modernity has deceived us into reading the Bible privately, individually, and rationalistically. What is needed in our day is a pilgrimage away from the academy and to the church. What is needed is a call to read the Bible publicly, communally, and theologically. Indeed, what is needed is Scripture. After all, man cannot live by texts and nutrients alone.

2

PLATO'S CAVE AND MR. ROGER'S NEIGHBORHOOD

I recently had a student get injured. Not seriously so, but enough to warrant a few sick days. I told the student I wanted to pray for her, that God would heal her ailment. She responded, "Thanks, but instead please pray that I'll be more faithful in having quiet times. I don't think God has much interest in my body, but I know he cares about my soul." I asked the student if she was able to do the readings from class while she was out. "Yes," she said hesitantly, "I've been up to my eyeballs in Plato!

Well over two millennia ago, Plato gave an analogy that helped shape much of Western philosophy going forward. Here's the most famous (though, not best) interpretation of the allegory: There are people in a dark cave facing a wall. Behind the people is a fire and behind the fire is an opening to the outside world. In that world, people walk, talk, dance, live.

Inside the cave, however, the people can only watch their shadows. Having never seen the outside, "real" world, the cave-people foolishly think the dancing shadows are ends in themselves, actual things. They aren't, of course; they're only shadows, "receptacles." Freedom, for Plato, is recognizing the ultimate vapidity and illusiveness of the material world. Physicality—"objects"—lie in the realm of mere opinion and shadow. It's in the incorporeal, metaphysical world of forms that true life can be found.

Having just completed readings surrounding this interpretation of the cave illustration, I asked the student, "how has this view shaped the church, do you think?" Substitute "objects" with "creation," "form-world" with "heaven," and you start to see the origin of the disembodied world many modern Christians inhabit. A view that leads us to think that only the spiritual world is real, and God takes no interest in concussions or broken bones.

This view stands in stark contrast with the biblical understanding of physicality. In Genesis 1 we see a world made by God. It is good, indeed, very good. Sin enters the world and distorts this goodness, but never eradicates the Creator's handiwork. Sin is like rust on a ship; it's not integral to the structure of the object. The ship existed before there was rust and will exist after the rust is removed. Indeed, the removal of the rust will only make the ship more of a ship.

The Christian view of creation can be seen well in this exchange between Mr. Rogers and one of his neighbors, Jeff Erlanger. Jeff was born with a tumor that left him bound to a wheelchair for the rest of his life. In the video, his handicap is pronounced and his young age only makes the disability more agonizing.

Watching the episode, I can see why Plato wanted to understand the world as mere shadow. It explains and relativizes so much of the torment and agony of life. In understanding ourselves as more than physicality, there is hope. However, what do we lose when we understand ourselves as less than physicality? While Plato's analogy can interpret our pain, I don't think it can account for the beauty and dignity of this world.

Mr. Rogers no doubt sees Jeff's brokenness, but he also sees his worth. To Jeff, he warmly sings, "It's you I like. Every part of you. Your skin, your eyes, your feelings." He saw the boy—the whole boy, body and soul—as real, as an end, as a creature. The wheelchair did not typify Jeff to Mr. Rogers.

Nor was the "real" Jeff simply his spirit. In that moment, Rogers did what he did so often; he recognized and named the humanity in the other. Jeff was not a shadow to Mr. Rogers, he was real, he was worthy, he was loved.

When recounting so many of the difficulties of being handicapped, Jeff reminds us that there is such difficulty for everyone, those inside and outside of wheelchairs. Jeff knows we are all on a scale of brokenness, all in need of healing in myriad ways. So, in addition to praying for my student's quiet times, I also prayed for her ailment, despite her earnest wishes.

Because denying the goodness of our bodies won't take away the badness. God did not place us in a cave, he placed us in a real-life neighborhood. The question is: will we see creation as a trick of the eye, or as a gift from the Creator? To do the former, ironically, is to choose to live in a cave of our own making. To do the later, however, is to be reminded of our Creator's love for his creation when we hear Mr. Rogers' song:

> It's you I like,
> It's not the things you wear,
> It's not the way you do your hair–
> But it's you I like
> The way you are right now,

The way down deep inside you–
Not the things that hide you,
Not your toys–
They're just beside you.
But it's you I like–
Every part of you,
Your skin, your eyes, your feelings
Whether old or new.
I hope that you'll remember
Even when you're feeling blue
That it's you I like,
It's you yourself,
It's you, it's you I like.

3

BABY DRIVER: GROWING UP NOSTALGIC

"An ethic unshaped by eschatology is neither Jesus' nor
Christian."
– Tremper Longman

HOW DOES an immature culture grow up? Edgar Wright's Baby
Driver is about the dangers of being lost in adolescence. By the
end of the movie, the viewer is pointed to a road we infer leads
to maturity, but only after a cinematically stunning tour de
force. The imbedded rhythm of the film sweeps one along from
scene to scene. The score follows the script—or vice versa—
ebbing and flowing in and out of dialog, music, and car chases
choreographed like masterful dance numbers.

The title star, "Baby," is the best getaway driver this side of
the Mississippi. Working for a man he owes (deftly played by
Kevin Spacey), Baby speeds one crew after another to safety
following each bank heist.

Baby has been living the Billy the Kid life since his mother and father were killed in a car wreck. Baby survives the crash, albeit with scars which he sees in the mirror and hears in his head. His tinnitus explains his ever-present ear buds, which helps drown out the ringing in his ears through a series of arduously arranged playlists.

As becomes evident, Baby is unable to mature beyond the accident. His independence on the road only accentuates the obvious fact that his whole life is one of unhealthy dependence upon his parents. He's still a child, still a baby; his identity fundamentally defined vis-à-vis his mom and dad. His parent's relationship was confrontational, he's pacifistic—letting Jamie Foxx's character abuse him with no recourse; his dad was a bad driver, he became a good driver; his mother sang, he lives in a musical world; she was a waitress, he can be found in her old diner day in and day out like a boy lost at a carnival returning to the last ride where he saw his parent.

Defining immaturity as *dependence* is a callback to an older era, matching the mid-century feel of the whole production. If Wright were trying to name a problem with our age, making Baby a prototype for overly dependent Millennials, he wouldn't be alone in his diagnosis. In his new book *The Vanishing American Adult*, Ben Sasse likewise sees the Achilles heel of the coming generation as their over reliance on others.

Following Jeffery Arnett's work on adolescence, Sasse uses the term, "self-focused age," referring to a time in life "when there are few real responsibilities, few 'daily obligations,' limited 'commitments to others.' In a stage when young people were once supposed to learn to 'stand alone as a self-sufficient person,' they find themselves increasingly paralyzed by over-choice." Put frankly, "Our kids simply don't know what an adult is anymore – or how to become one. Many don't even see a reason to try." Thus, Millennials are trapped in perpetual adolescence; a decadent, morbidly self-gratifying state in which one consumes more than contributes.

The crux of Sasse's advice is simple, "roll up your sleeves!" His own daughter, as an example, spent a summer working on a ranch, learning life lessons about hard work, responsibility, and self-reliance. She takes ownership of her own life, her own actions, her own income. This is also the lesson Baby has to learn.

In the climactic scene in which Baby is running away from the law with his lover, he surprisingly surrenders. He throws the key to the car off a bridge, lifts his hands, goes to court, then prison, and serves his time. With his ear buds out and his cars impounded, he confronts life for himself, taking responsibility for his actions. He makes a new life, which may not be as glamorous as his old, but is his nonetheless.

The movie ends ambiguously in a black and white shot with Baby's girlfriend picking him up in a vintage car, wearing a poodle skirt, seeming to embody the romance and innocence of 1950's Americana. Whether this scene is a fantasy is left to interpretation, but the implication is clear: if only Baby could go back to a time before he was born, before his parents were born, then he could gain complete independence from his and their sins.

Sasse also wants us to go back, "Many Americans coming of age today don't understand the country they're inheriting." So let's get back to our roots, argues Sasse. Let's throw the keys off the bridge, live within our means, make an honest living, and get to know the American experiment in which we find ourselves. To go forward, we actually need to go backward, as Baby did.

Back to where? To which age? Sasse is clear not only in his

book, but in his media appearances and speeches as well: "American exceptionalism is a claim about what happened in the American founding, and if we don't understand why the American founding was extraordinary, you can be sure that our kids won't understand why America is extraordinary." Sasse's remedy is tied up in what he calls "civic catechesis;" an immersion in the primary sources of American liberty.

To be sure, America's founding was extraordinary, and we would be fools not to retrieve wisdom from any and every age. Yet, I'm sensitive of the temptation to make any bygone era the cure-all for our modern ills. When I hear sentiments akin to "Make America Great Again," I always question: even if we could go back twenty years or two hundred years, what would keep the exact same problems from coming back again?

For example, might there be a connection between those today that believe they can choose their own gender and those of yesteryear who prioritized the individual's will? This is not meant to be a slight upon the founding fathers, only an admission of the obvious: maturity is found by going to the future, not the past.

It's incumbent upon the church, now more than ever, to be a beacon of such forward-looking maturity, a witness not to some golden age of the past, but to the age to come. This passage from Moby Dick offers a clarion call:

"The pulpit is ever this earth's foremost part; all the rest comes in its rear; the pulpit leads the world... Yes, the world's a ship on its passage out, and not a voyage complete; and the pulpit is its prow."

Too often, the pulpit assumes a lesser place on the ship of society. Rather than casting a fresh vision of human flourishing, we look to the past with rose-colored glasses, believing if we could only go back we'd do it differently, we'd do it right; we'd stay the course.

None of this is to say either Baby Driver or *The Vanishing American Adult* are inherently flawed; only that, given our current political mood, both can be wrongly used to justify a wistful, naïve understanding of perpetual adolescence's cause and remedy. Christians must balk against any idea that our salvation will come driving a 1950's Cadillac or a 1770's chariot. Through the life, death, resurrection, and ascension of Jesus, the future is invading the present. Maturity lies ahead, not behind.

4

ART IN GOD'S GOOD WORLD

But if you confess that the world was once beautiful, but by the curse has become undone, and by a final catastrophe is to pass to its full state of glory, excelling even the beauty of paradise, then art has the mystical task of reminding us in its production of the beauty that was lost and of anticipating its perfect coming luster. - Abraham Kuyper

"WHAT CHARACTER WOULD I eliminate if I wrote this?" That's a question I ask myself after finishing every book. When I first started asking this question, villains came to mind: Grendel's mother, Claudius, Sauron – the bad guys.

Of course, the older I get the more I realize how boring fiction would be without antagonists. Who would read Harry Potter were it not for Voldemort, after all? The answers I give to that question have shifted from those who create the most conflict in the story to those who create the least; bit characters, vanilla sidekicks.

ART IN GOD'S World Involves Beauty Born of Tension

WHILE THIS EXERCISE may seem silly, it actually develops a necessary skill for the evaluation of any piece of art, written or otherwise: the ability to identify and appreciate tension. Beauty, especially beauty seen in the arts, is the result of tension, of one kind or another.

Obviously, the kind of tension that typically comes to mind is that between good and bad, right and wrong: Aslan and the White Witch. Christianity gives a full-throated voice to this tension.

While the world was created good, it is fallen – which is to say it's both broken and rebellious – but Christ has come to restore and redeem creation. In other words, Christ has come to resolve this tension.

This story of Creation, Fall, and Redemption permeates the Scriptures, and because the Scriptures tell the true story of this world, it permeates our experience as well. Thus, for art to be affirmed by the Christian worldview, it of course can – and must – touch on these themes.

Granted, each and every piece of art won't include each and every theme each and every time. A work that reflects the pain and depravity of creation is no less true than the work that points to the world's inherent dignity and goodness, or a work that alludes to the balm and remedy brought by Christ, for that matter.

· · ·

Is Beauty Eternal?

THE FACT that beauty is a result of tension – and the tension between good and evil is resolvable – poses an interesting and important question vis-à-vis the Christian aesthetic; namely, "is beauty eternal?"

The answer is more complex than one might first expect. The tension between "good" and "bad" is contingent upon evil, which is finite. Obviously, before the Fall and after the second coming of Christ, there is no such tension. This tension has a beginning (Gen 3) and an end (Rev 21).

At least the three Abrahamic religions (Christianity, Judaism, and Islam) agree on this point: evil is not eternal. It has a beginning and an end. This tension will be resolved. But the Christian faith has a unique claim on beauty specifically.

Before the Fall, indeed before Creation, God lived in perfect love, peace, joy, and relationship. The Father, the Son, and the Spirit were one, yet three. Were God only one – were he a mono-personal being – there would be no tension in eternity past, let alone in the perfect world to come.

God is not such a being. While we can affirm the "oneness" of God's essence, we can also affirm the various personalities of the Trinity. This tension between Father, Son, and Spirit is irresolvable. It is the governing reality of the cosmos. Of course, this reality is why we can say that love is eternal. There has always been "love," a "lover," and a "beloved."

This is also why Christians can say beauty is eternal. Before the creation of the world, God was not stagnant. He was in a complex and textured relationship with his Trinitarian self. Tension is eternal because of the eternality of the Trinity.

· · ·

AT ITS BEST, Art Makes Us Worship

DAVID SKEEL ALLUDES to this very matter in his book *True Paradox*. As Trinitarians, Skeel argues, we can heartily acknowledge there are more tensions in the world than those between "good" and "bad." When we look at a truly beautiful painting, we appreciate the tension not only between right and wrong, but also between colors, shades, fabrics, etc. These tensions – those that exist apart from sin – allude to the complexity found in the Godhead.

This is why a given piece of art can have such a transcendent effect on the viewer. In viewing beauty, as with experiencing love, the connoisseur is coming in contact with something that lacks a beginning and an end. At its best, this is what art does. Art makes us worship – not the object, of course, but the reality that lies beyond the object: the Triune God of the universe.

5

THE ESCHATOLOGY OF DOWNTON ABBEY

L ongtime fans of *Downton Abbey* probably guessed that the show would end with a Christmas special. And they were right; at least, partly right. To be more precise, Downton ended on New Year's Day, 1926. It turns out, the series finale was less about endings and more about beginnings. It was about the dawn of new age, a new order. It was about the Kingdom come. Indeed, it pointed to the Christian gospel: Christ is not ending the world, but making it new.

Exile

The episode began with most of its characters in a resigned estrangement. Edith and Bertie, for example, are still not speaking. Edith withheld the fact that Marigold was more than her ward, she was her daughter. Upon learning their true relation, Bertie promptly said his goodbyes. Within the first few minutes of the episode, Edith referred to herself as a "spinster" and "damaged goods," destined to live a lonely, husbandless existence in her London apartment.

Thomas the footman is beyond Downton's property for the first time in years, having been pressured into taking a position at a house far less regal and familial. His new benefactors obviously don't care for him; he's simply their butler, an employee of the estate. Like Edith's mess, this exile could have been avoided. From the beginning, Thomas' wounds were self-inflicted (remember how he got a built in his hand?). His conniving and manipulation did him no favors as he now longed for the castle over the hills.

Because of their deceit, Edith and Thomas lost the only thing which could bring them satisfaction: Edith was without love and Thomas without home. This is always the path of sin. In rebelling against the order of the house—in trying to manipulate the system to gain power—Thomas was like Adam and Eve who were not content with the just rule of paradise.

They didn't want God dictating right and wrong to them, they wanted autonomy—a kingdom of their own law. In trying to hide her daughter, Edith was also like Adam and Eve: hidden, shamed, isolated. Of course, our first parents eventually shared in Thomas' expulsion: exiled from the garden, driven away from home. The house in which they now served was hard—thorns and blisters abounded. A smiling Father was traded for a scowling master.

Return

The question of Downton—the question which Mr. Carson was never able to stomach—was always: How can we adapt to the changing world? How do the ethics of the new age relate to the systems of the old? Put simply, how will we have a happy ending? The answer, it turns out, is simple: we walk into the new world humbly.

Thomas was a footman in the Abbey, and he resented that fact. He did everything in his power to move, even ever so slightly, up the ladder. He lied. He cheated. He blackmailed. He bribed. The end of all Thomas' scheming came this season in a bloody bathtub with his wrists slit. While he was rescued, he was still not invited to make his home at Downton.

That background sets the stage for perhaps the most moving scene in the finale. Mr. Carson's "palsy" prevents him from properly pouring the champagne, and it becomes obvious that his days as butler are over. These circumstances—which Thomas could not have orchestrated—lead to Mary's nominating the estranged footman for the job. While he's at his least powerful—indeed, while he's completely estranged from the family—he's mercifully invited back into the fellowship. Not based on something of his own doing, but wholly based on Lady Mary's favor and mercy. Forevermore Thomas' service in the home will be a testament not to his trademark ambition or merit, but to the Crawley's grace.

Just as Thomas was able to go home in humility, so too did Edith receive love vulnerably. Weddings are always eschatological events in the Christian understanding of things. The bride is a pointer to the church and Christ is the ultimate Bridegroom. One day, the institution of marriage will fade like a shadow as the substance—Christ and his bride—are united. We go into that day the same way Edith went into her wedding: vulnerably. For the first time Edith was completely honest.

To her fiancé, to her soon-to-be mother-in-law, to herself. As the minister asked if there were any objections to their nuptials, there was silence. There were no secrets left—Edith had shared them all. She was known fully for the first time, and loved anyway. The love given to Edith was just that, given. It was a gift. It was grace. Such is the love which will bring in the Kingdom.

We can never demand love, we can only receive it—after all, we, like Edith, have betrayed the trust of our Bridegroom. That great wedding feast is coming in grace, in love. The Kingdom will not come in protests or in riots or in persuasive speeches. The Kingdom does not come by demanding bread and wine, but by receiving the elements.

The Kingdom does not come by the church covering her shame and nakedness with the vapid leaves of power and influence, but in prayer and service to the poor. Like Thomas, we go home not based on our own merits, but on the grace of our master. Like Edith, we don't look for our wedding day as if it's owed to us, but we look as those waiting on a gift. Which is to say: we wait humbly.

Shalom

From the show's inception, two worlds are taken for granted: the upstairs world and the downstairs world. The basic tension of the series lies in the two worlds dissolving into one another. Upstairs is moving downstairs (think early on of Lady Mary's going down to the servants quarters to talk with Carson) and downstairs is moving upstairs (think of Tom, the driver and mechanic, moving up to marry Lady Sybil).

This is typified in the closing minutes of Downton's finale, which could not have be more different than the opening minutes of the show's pilot. After going into labor, the ultimate servants, Anna and John Bates, lie upstairs in Lady Mary's bed as tea is served to them by Lord Grantham himself. The old order has passed away. Baby Bates is delivered along with a new age, a new rule.

This scene sums up the plot of Downton well. Anna and John had a hard time conceiving a child. To Anna, it seemed impossible at times. This new birth came only through much pain, sorrow, and heartache. That's the eschatology of Downton Abbey: resurrection comes through the cross. New life comes through the painful death of the old.

Watching a century after the fact, the death of this bygone aristocratic era seemed imminent. If the advent of the automobile and telephone didn't quite usher in the new age, the Great War surely did. Nothing could be the same. How much more so should the coming Kingdom of Christ seem inevitable? After all, we're watching our present drama play out some two millennia after the Kingdom was decisively secured by Christ's life, death, resurrection, and ascension.

The writers of Downton are clearly emboldened by their belief in the inevitable "march of progress." Yet, the Christian gospel offers something different, something more. History is under the sovereign rule of Christ: it has a telos. So we walk humbly into the future, receiving the Kingdom as a gift. We live in this present "kingdom of darkness" with the sure knowledge that its day is setting, even as the "Kingdom of light" is dawning. In the end, Downton offers a glimmer of our Christian eschatology of hope. To quote Isobel Crawley in the closing words of the series: "We are going forward to the future, not back in the past." From Eden, to the New Jerusalem. Amen.

6

BEAUTY AND THE MARK OF THE BEAST

"Winter turns to spring / Famine turns to feast / Nature points the way / Nothing left to say / Beauty and the Beast." –Mrs. Potts

"Sleep is an image of death that is repeated every night. So the morning is the image of the resurrection. So the spring of the year is an image of the resurrection." –Jonathan Edwards

HOW WILL the dark curse be broken? Sacrificial love. In the stunning new remake of *Beauty and the Beast*, Disney stayed true to this central theme. And why shouldn't they? After all, it's a "tale as old as time," the story of resurrection and the path thereunto. Indeed, the curse being broken by love is *the* story of all time, true as it can be.

As the story goes, the curse leveled by the beggar-woman in the opening scene is death, though not an obvious sort of death. Those under the curse, while turned to dishware and furniture, can still move and speak. But they are somehow not themselves–the longer they live under the curse, the less themselves they become.

It's hard to hear Mr. Clocksworth's lament, "I feel myself becoming less human" without being aware of our own inhumanity. Who hasn't felt like a shadow of themselves? Even if one doesn't believe in the deep magic found in Scripture, who hasn't nevertheless longed for the spell under which we live to be broken?

The only path back to life is love, and Belle—the stranger held captive in the castle—is lovely. Naturally, the creatures of the house seek to charm Belle into love. Likewise, the Beast bangs on the door, demanding a romantic dinner. But love can't come this way.

Ironically, love comes when Belle is released from captivity; as she runs away from the property back to her father. In a beautiful scene on the castle's balcony, Belle asks the Beast, "Can anyone truly love who isn't free?" At that, the Beast turns Belle away. By the end of the movie, the Beast and his entire castle staff die. And Belle weeps.

While Belle is good, she's not giving herself to the Beast, not yet anyway. Taking her life-giving kiss—which she only offers at the end of the movie—without first sending her away would have been temporary security, but a final sort of death ultimately. On the balcony, the Beast understands a deep mystery; love will come through *loneliness*, pleasure through *pain*. So he sends Belle away and walks into the darkness.

In Scripture, life always comes through death. The way up is down. Commenting on *Revelation*, Peter Leithart makes the easily missed point that *seal* and *mark* are juxtaposed from one another. Those 144,000 people *sealed* by God in chapter 7 are set-aside for death. Those with the *mark* of the beast in chapter 13, however, are free to buy and sell goods—they feast, they live. Says Leithart:

"Those who do not receive the mark of the beast do die, but their death is a passage to renewed life. The unmarked, those sealed for death, rise again and reign with Christ. The mark of the beast rescued from immediate death, but the important things don't happen at the beginning. We only know what the marks and the seals mean when we get to the end of things."

It's obvious why the mark of the beast is so attractive; it offers immediate salvation (or satisfaction). It gives us the sustenance and safety needed to see another day. To be clear, these things aren't bad in and of themselves. On the contrary, food, drink, life—these are good, but they are by nature gifts, and gifts aren't gifts if ripped from the giver's hand.

They must be received, not taken. Love requires as much. In the end, there is a feast for those who refuse the mark of the beast, but only through famine. There is resurrection, but only through death. Seeking the Kingdom apart from the cross is not only counterproductive; it's satanic (Mt 4:8). So, we seek the seal of God, not the mark of the beast, come what may.

Upon her return, Belle brings more than tears to the ransacked castle; she brings new life. From her lips comes resurrection, breaking the curse once and for all. In a grand celebratory feast, she dances with her lover who is now, at long last, transformed into who he was always supposed to be. When the Beast sent Belle away, he planted the painful seed of death. At the dance, we see death's fruit: life.

Beauty and the Beast and *Revelation* have the same counterintuitive message: if you want to save your life, lose your life. You cannot force redemption. You must die, and wait. In the hope that we will all be raised back to ourselves again—humanity fully restored. At that grand banquet, there will be no doubt: the dark curse is broken under the foot of sacrificial love.

7

BEATRIZ AT DINNER: SALVATION THROUGH HOSPITALITY

Behold, I stand at the door and knock. If anyone hears my voice and opens the door, I will come in to him and eat with him, and he with me. –Jesus, Revelation 3:20

THE OLD HYMN COMMANDS, "let every heart prepare him room!" This is what a Christian is, after all: one who has welcomed Jesus. *Welcoming* has been part and parcel of Christian faith and practice since the beginning—first century Christians adopting diseased children, Paul instructing Philemon to receive his former slave back home as a brother, Jesus eating with the outcast, Israel welcoming the sojourners. Even if it isn't easy to do, we can at least understand how to show hospitality to the weak and vulnerable. But God is not weak or vulnerable. How do we open the door of our lives to him? How do we "make him room?"

Mark tells the story (1:35-39) of Jesus being perfectly disciplined. He gets up early, he prays, he orders his time based on God's mission rather than the opinions and needs of others. What does it look like to show hospitality to one so whole, so absent of need? Miguel Arteta's beautiful new film Beatriz at Dinner gives us a clue. After her car breaks down at the home of a client, Beatriz—a new age massage therapist and holistic healer—finds herself stranded at an upscale dinner party.

At first glance, the movie is a contrast between Beatriz (Salma Hayek) and Doug (John Lithgow), a high-powered businessman. He is invited to dinner, the guest of honor, she is unexpected; he's everyone's employer, she's an employee to his employee; he boasts, she demurs; he takes life—showing pictures of his prize kill from a recent safari expedition, she gives life.

Early in the movie, Beatriz weeps as she recounts that an angry neighbor killed her pet goat—"murder." Throughout the dinner, Beatriz swears she recognizes Doug. Was he the man who built a hotel in her hometown that displaced a swath of the community? No, he's too young. But how *does* she know him? By the end of the party, after proclaiming, "all tears come from the same source," she looks Doug in the eye and mater-of-factly states, "you killed my goat." On one level, the movie is about the conflict between good and evil.

The brilliance of the film, however, is found not in the leads, but in the near perfectly cast team of character-actors around the dinner table. As two radically opposing forces collide, we see tension, deflection, amusement, and horror in the onlooker's faces. At its heart, Beatriz at Dinner isn't about Beatriz or Doug at all; it's about the guests at the dinner party, and the choice they'll all have to make by the end of the evening. On the one hand, Doug offers power. Beatriz, conversely, offers the promise of healing, and healing in a way particular to each of them: cancer in one case, back-pain in another.

As the evening progresses, it becomes evident that what Doug and Beatriz have to offer is mutually exclusive. To whom will each guest show hospitality, Doug or Beatriz? While the woman who first insisted Beatriz come to the party attempts to straddle the fence, she too is forced to take sides. To get Doug's approval, the guests must grovel—they must earn their place around the table. They can't seem weak or vulnerable. They are valuable to Doug insofar as they're useful, but not a minute longer. At one point, he jokes about leaving his third wife for a more attractive guest at the party.

Beatriz's gift, however, is just that: a gift. It can't be earned, only received. The difficulty, the predicament, the tragedy, is that no one can let down their pretense and airs to see their need—not now, not at a party, not when so much is at stake. To take hold of the hope Beatriz can offer (the unseen) requires abandoning that which Doug is currently offering (the seen). Alas, one can't serve two masters.

Back to the Gospel of Mark. After describing how Jesus is whole, Mark immediately tells the story of a man who is broken (1: 40-45). When he encounters Jesus, the man isn't told, as you might expect, to find healing by doing the good things Jesus just did. He's not asked to earn his place in Jesus' presence; he isn't told how to pull himself up by his bootstraps. Rather, Jesus reaches down, out of pity, and heals the man of his leprosy directly. By running to Jesus the man was running away from every other form of salvation; he came bringing only his need, and that was enough.

Like Beatriz, Jesus joyfully comes to dinner, bringing healing with him. However, it's not a given that we will welcome him. To the contrary, welcoming Jesus involves the painful, uncertain process of letting go of our pride and self-satisfaction. By showing hospitality to Jesus we're necessarily neglecting those other masters in our lives who demand our complete loyalty and attention. Jesus stands at the door and knocks, ready to dine with us. How do we welcome him? One hymn tells us to "make him room;" another hymn—reminiscent of Beatriz at Dinner—tells us how:

"COME, ye weary, heavy laden, bruised and broken by the fall; if you tarry 'til you're better, you will never come at all.... Let not conscience make you linger, nor of fitness fondly dream; all the fitness He requires is to feel your need of Him."

8

MUST HOLIDAYS BE HOLY?

"Your drink has been paid for." The barista spilled a bit of coffee as she explained the random act of kindness, "The car in front of you took care of your order—the driver told me to tell you Merry Christmas!" It was a small gesture, but a strangely meaningful one for me in that moment. "Wow! Thank you! Merry Christmas to her and to you also!" The barista's response stayed with the rest of the day, "You know, it's sad that such kindness has to be tied to Christmas— as if we can only show mercy and generosity toward one another because of a holiday."

Surely she was right, can't we find ways to be more humane toward one another even when Bing Crosby isn't playing on the radio every half hour? But I also had doubts, doubts that I nursed throughout the day. Sure, one can be charitable and kind while totally rejecting the Christmas message, we all know people like that. Yet, are such acts intelligible in what Peter Jones calls a "Oneist" view of the world? That is, if there is no

"Other," no God distinct from his creation, do our graceful acts make sense? I don't think so, and neither do many of the sharpest Oneist thinkers, like Friedrich Nietzsche.

For Nietzsche, virtues like grace, mercy, and kindness are "merely an honorable form of stupidity." Those who practice them simply "project their own honorable stupidity and goodness into the heart of things." The "things" to which Nietzsche refers is the mystery of the universe—God, namely. A loving God is the work of fiction produced by the sentimental pining of a kind person. Our internal kindness simply gets reflected back onto the external world—next thing you know, there is a God willing to forgive sins. And it goes the other way around as well, if there is a kind God who shows mercy, then it's incumbent upon his children to pass along such charity. (i.e. "forgive us our trespasses as we forgive those who trespass against us.")

"We others" says Nietzsche speaking on behalf of his fellow atheists, "we read something else into the heart of things: our own enigmatic nature, our contradictions, our deeper, more painful, more mistrustful wisdom." Just as the vitreous people live lives in harmony with external reality, so too does Nietzsche want harmony: if life is pointless, dark, and cold, the only meaning to be found is in what we make for ourselves, in what he calls our "will to power."

Nietzsche pointed to particular men in history who exemplified such will—the Übermensch, the Superman. These men sacrificed, worked tirelessly, strove beyond their fellowmen to gain for themselves power, and with power purpose, and with purpose dignity, and with dignity worth. This is the path to meaning in such a worldview: advance yourself, beat others to the top of whatever hill you decide to climb, win at all costs.

You can start to see why Nietzsche had antipathy for the Christian ethic. The Apostle Paul gives the exact opposite instruction to the church at Philippi, "Do nothing from selfish ambition or conceit," he says," but in humility count others more significant than yourselves. Let each of you look not only to his own interests, but also to the interests of others."

Rather than *will to power*, one almost expects Paul to coin the phrase, *will to service*. And why should we act in such a counterintuitive way? Paul answers by pointing to the life Jesus, our savior who "though he was in the form of God, did not count equality with God a thing to be grasped, but emptied himself, by taking the form of a servant, being born in the likeness of men. And being found in human form, he humbled himself by becoming obedient to the point of death, even death on a cross."

For Paul, selflessness isn't a given, it isn't born in a vacuum, it's born in a manger. You see, at Christmas we celebrate the ultimate anti-Übermensch story: Jesus left the throne room of Heaven to be born in a cave as a poor refugee. As he grew older, he had no place to lay his head. He suffered under Pontius Pilate, he was crucified, he died, he was buried. His arduous journey was downward, from Heaven to Hell. He didn't sacrifice himself so that he might gain power, he sacrificed his power so that he might give to others—meaning, purpose, dignity, all the things Nietzsche tried to make for himself but couldn't. Nietzsche's "God is dead" creed can never inspire the generosity that Nicaea's "God is alive and coming back" creed can.

In my estimation, Nietzsche's worldview makes perfect sense if we do indeed live in a godless world. If there is no God, we're left to strive, take, and conquer our neighbors. To find significance we have to look inward. But if the Christmas message is true, then by looking outside of ourselves, to the person and work of Christ, the Christmas spirit—joy, peace, mercy—is available to us year-round. Because he was denied a room in the inn, we can live lives of radical hospitality. Because our worth isn't found in what we take, we're free to give—gifts to our friends and family, and coffee to strangers behind us at a Starbucks drive thru. The Christmas spirit is incomprehensible apart from the Christmas story.

9

COME AND SEE: THE END GOAL OF APOLOGETICS

The heart is not changed by argument, the heart is changed by divine intervention. – Ravi Zacharias

HOW LONG AFTER becoming a Christian should one wait before engaging in apologetics? Three years? Four? The disciple Philip waited only two verses! In John 1:43 Philip becomes a follower of Christ. In verse 45, he's found sharing the gospel with Nathanael!

Listening for the question behind the question

Then as now, sharing the gospel was met with skepticism. Nathanael's doubt revolved around Jesus' hometown, "Can anything good come out of Nazareth?" While Nathanael's question may seem straightforward, it's more complex than it first appears. This is typically the case in evangelistic encounters.

All skeptics enter into theological discussions with myriad interests, backgrounds, and wounds. To truly address their question, one must truly hear their question. That is, one must listen with the goal of understanding, not just the goal of responding. This requires as much love as learning, as much empathy as answers. In Nathanael's case, his question regarding Jesus' hometown has at least two aspects: cultural and theological.

A cultural objection: Nazareth isn't Jerusalem

Culturally, Nazareth was an out of the way, nowhere town. How could the long awaited Messiah be found in such a seemingly insignificant place? The good news is always proclaimed in seeming weakness (I Cor. 2:1-2).

While the gospel is vast and cosmic—Christ redeeming all of creation—the means of fulfilling the promise are quite humble: preaching, sacraments, small acts of mercy and grace, and similarly obscure acts.

Resurrection is brought about through the cross. In Nathanael's question, we're pricked with the sting of scorn. We stand vulnerable with Philip, proclaiming a message we know to be so large, yet seems so small and culturally insignificant in the moment.

A theological objection: Nazareth isn't Bethlehem

As a Jewish believer, Nathanael would no doubt have been interested in Philip's claim that he had found "the one of whom Moses and the Prophets spoke." Yet while Moses and the Prophets say much about the coming savior, they say nothing about Nazareth. While those of us familiar with the

Christmas story can understand how Jesus was both "from Bethlehem" and "of Nazareth," the question of the Messiah's origin had likely not crossed Phillip's mind in his two-verse-tenure as a Christian. And so it will be with our apologetic encounters.

Questions will be posed to us that we'll never have previously considered. Questions of Christ's deity and humanity, questions of the Bible's origin, questions of church history to do with the Crusades, Christian involvement in the slave trade, etc. It should never take us off guard that non-believers have such daunting questions. The Christian faith is one of paradox and nuance, and it's lived out by imperfect, often contradictory people.

Come and See!

With such a question on the table—one evoking matters of class, culture, and theology—one might expect the young Christian to ask for a few days to research and investigate before offering the exact right response. But in lieu of an answer, Phillip gives Nathanael something better; he gives him an invitation, "come and see!" Nathanael wanted to stand in judgment over Jesus—evaluating this or that fact. But even if Philip had been able to answer this and all of Nathanael's questions point for point, Nathanael needed more than points, he needed a person, whether he knew it or not.

As Nathanael approaches, Jesus doesn't immediately offer answers, though no doubt he saw the questions in his face. Instead, Jesus proclaims "I saw you under the fig tree." Perhaps Nathanael prayed under a fig tree as a child, or maybe he was under a fig tree that morning. In any case, Nathanael's doubts turned to awe. He thought he would believe only if he could know, but he began to believe once he had been known. He came to see, he left having been seen.

Eventually, as he grew to know Jesus more, Philip would be able to answer the question posed by Nathanael. However, I'm sure his response to non-believers never changed, "come and see!" Because the goal of apologetics is more than the dissemination of facts, it's the invitation into a relationship. It's the possibility of knowing and being known. It's an encounter with the living Christ. Come and see!

10

THE WHOLE BIBLE IN ONE VERSE

When asked which verse best summarizes the whole of Scripture, Edmund Clowney famously pointed to Jonah 2:9, "Salvation belongs to the LORD." I've heard Bryan Chapell answer a similar question with the same verse. In terms of one verse standing on its own, I doubt a better answer could be given.

If context is considered, though, I'd argue a better summation of Scripture comes two verses later: "Then the word of the LORD came to Jonah a second time" (Jonah 3:1).

Down, Down, Down

The word initially came to Jonah while he was in the promised land. While enjoying the peace and security of Yahweh's presence, he was told to prophesy to the Assyrians. In a sense, Jonah was called to extend the boundaries of Yahweh's rule from the little territory of Israel to the "exceedingly great city" of Nineveh.

From here, we know the story. Jonah rebels against the initial word. He goes down toward Tarshish, he goes down in the ship, he goes down in the fish, and is finally "driven from the sight of the LORD." While in the belly of the fish Jonah laments the fact that he's far from the temple, far from the presence of God. Rebellion against the first word brought exile from the temple; it brought spiritual death.

We can say Jonah 3:1 sums up Scripture since the Jonah story mirrors the biblical story in significant ways. In the beginning, God created the world through his word. Adam and Eve received the good creation brought about through this "first word." Like Jonah, they lived in the peace and security of Yahweh's presence. The land in which they lived functioned as a little "temple-garden." Their mission: extend the boundaries of the garden over the face of the earth. They were called to bring the order of the inner garden to the entire world, just as Jonah was called to bring the message of God's order and justice to this foreign nation.

Though Adam and Eve didn't experience immediate physical death when they rebelled against the first word, they were driven from the Lord's presence. No, they weren't in the belly of a fish. But they were banished from the garden-temple. This was their "going down," this was their death, just as it was Jonah's.

Evangelism Explosion

God would've been perfectly just to end the story there. He was under no obligation to speak his creative word the first time, let alone a second. God could have destroyed his creation. Yet, in his grace and providence, he established a plan to inaugurate a "new creation." How was this new creation to come about? The same way in which the old creation came into existence: through the word. Inexplicably, the word came to mankind a second time.

No, a second spoken word didn't come. Rather, the same word—the word by which God had crafted the world—came again, this time in flesh and blood. Jesus Christ had a clear mission: extend the temple presence of Yahweh over the face of the whole earth. God sent his incarnate Word into the world so that all things might be new, that salvation might explode over the face of the earth.

This expansive mission is what the returned word to Jonah was all about. The rest of Jonah 3 tells the story of a foreign people, including their king, repenting and "believing God" (Jonah 3:5). To Jonah's surprise (and dismay), God had plans for the world that didn't end with Israel.

This "returned word" had a much bigger scope than Jonah had anticipated. It accounted for the far-off city of Nineveh. Indeed, it even accounted for Nineveh's cattle (Jonah 4:11). This was an expansive, inclusive, all-encompassing word.

Sign of Jonah

Of course, the story of a first and second word can't sum up the Bible's story any more than it can sum up Jonah's story. To know Jonah, you must know the story of his going down and coming up from the fish.

And to know the story of Scripture, you must understand Jesus's decent and ascent from the grave. In between the rebellion of the world and the radical salvation offered to the ends of the earth, there stands a chosen Israelite (Jonah 1:1–2; Matt. 1:23).

While it seems he's delivered to death solely by the hands of men (Jonah 1:15; John 19:17–37), God is actually the primary agent of this Israelite's death, according to his definite plan and foreknowledge (Jonah 2:3; Acts 2:23). Death could not contain this man, however, and after three days he was resurrected from the deep (Jonah 2:10; Luke 24:1–12).

This resurrected Israelite stood in the city of evildoers, announcing the way of reconciliation (Jonah 3:4; Luke 24:27). "God's wrath may be spared," he announced. "Repent and believe, for God's word has come again!"

THE STORY OF JONAH—THE story of Scripture—is the story of:

1. The Word given.
2. Rebellion against the Word.
3. Death and resurrection.
4. The Word returning to extend the rule of God wider, longer, and deeper than anyone could have imagined.

IF WE LOOK CLOSELY, Jonah 3:1 not only summarizes Scripture, it summarizes our experience as believers. By nature we were each rebels against the Word—Assyrians by birth. Like the sailors, and like the Roman soldiers, we're implicated in the death of the chosen Israelite.

Yet each of us heard the good news—that Christ was thrown overboard so the storm of God's judgment might pass over our boat. Because Christ went down into the belly of death —cut off from the presence of the Lord—we can have eternal temple access. Along with Jonah, we can gladly announce the good news, "The word of the LORD came a second time!"

11

THE FOOLISHNESS OF STEPHEN COLBERT

"We're very opposite." That's what Bill Maher said to Stephen Colbert in a recent interview. In the conversation—which ranged from mildly awkward, to tense, to nearing hostile—Maher and Colbert take turns sharing jabs about the other's opinion on the proper response to global terrorism, the presidential election, and religion.

However, despite Maher's claim to the contrary, the tension in the conversation was not, in fact, due to a difference of opinion—it was not because they are "opposites." Rather, the tension was a result of a belief Maher and Colbert share, something upon which they profoundly agree. Both Maher and Colbert recognize the all-encompassing scope of Christ's claims. Both understand that Christ's lordship extends past the four walls of a church and reaches into the public square, the body politic.

Perhaps a little context will help here, though Maher's view on religion hardly needs to be recounted. He's built a whole cottage industry on mocking faith and the faithful. In his 2008 documentary *Religulous,* he left no stone unturned in his pursuit to find the weakest arguments for faith. In the end, he made the following conclusion:

"The plain fact is religion must die for mankind to live. The hour is getting very late to be able to indulge in having key decisions made by religious people – by irrationalists – by those who would steer the ship of state, not by a compass, but by the equivalent of reading the entrails of a chicken."

Maher's sentiment is strong; he hedges no bets. Like many of the so called "new atheists," Maher does not want the religious and the irreligious to "play nice," or even go their separate ways. No, Maher sees religion as a malignant cancer in need of eradication. To be clear, it's not only those acts of violence committed in the name of religion which Maher decries, it's religion itself.

Maher understands that religious beliefs cannot be contained—they cannot be hermetically sealed from the rest of one's thought and behavior. Religion, in Maher's estimation, is a menace to society precisely because it cannot be properly "private." Faith is inherently "public" because it claims to define truth, goodness, beauty, and indeed all of reality. Thus, we can't have people serving food, much less holding public office, who hold such convictions. After all, who knows when and where those beliefs might come out?

As infamous as Maher's views are to those with faith, Colbert's are nearly as bad to those without. In an interview with the Catholic media outlet *Salt and Light,* Colbert was asked about how one balances religion with one's political life. Colbert dismissed the question out of hand. He balked, "There is no need to balance them!" In explaining what he meant, he quoted

Thomas More's line in *A Man for all Seasons*, "Those who abandon their faith for the sake of their public duties will lead their country by a short route to chaos." After quoting the line, Colbert asks, "What else do we have to inform our public life other than our conscience?" Of course, the implication is that our conscience is informed by our faith, thus our faith has direct application to the whole of life, including political life.

It's clear that neither Maher nor Colbert are likely to pick up a "coexist" sticker for their laptop. Both comedians understand the comprehensive claim being made by various faiths. All can't be true; all can't be equal. Each worldview—including Maher's atheism—makes a claim that is exclusive.

This clarifies the subtext in the aforementioned interview. It explains the downright awkward feel of the whole thing. Bill can't say "you do you!" to Stephen any more than Stephen can say "to each his own!" to Bill. Both men are drawing up borders which leaves the other on the "outside." Both are representatives of kingdoms making the exact same claim on the exact same sphere. For either to capitulate with a "if that works for you..." sentiment would be paramount to treason.

Thus, the only way there can be resolution—the only way to relieve the tension—is for one party to concede, to join the other party. Our multicultural, egalitarian sensibilities don't much care for such "either/or" ultimatums. It's uncomfortable. It's abrasive. It smacks of a medieval authoritarianism abandoned long ago for a more enlightened inclusivism. Yet both players in the interview understand the game, and both are competing to win.

Colbert offers Maher Pascal's wager: If you believe the gospel and it turns out to be false, you're an idiot. If you don't believe and it turns out to be true, you're going to hell. Colbert understands that Maher—along with most of the audience—thinks Christianity is wrong. If Colbert's faith is wrong, by his own reckoning, he's an idiot. In everyone's eyes Colbert is a clown, a fool—but he's a fool for Christ.

Just before taking on CBS's *Late Night*, Colbert famously said "To be a fool for Christ is to love." I'm not sure I fully understood what Colbert meant by this until his Maher interview. Colbert could have resolved the tension with Maher in a different way. He could've laughed off the question of faith and made an easy Trump joke, but that's not what he did. He embraced the tension. He entered into the foolishness. He told Maher that, outside of Christ, he was bound for hell.

Why? Why did Colbert chose to resolve the tension by inviting Maher back to church, back to fellowship with Christ and his people? Colbert tells us: love. Had he been motivated by, say, peace, he could've saved face and changed the subject. For the sake of peace he could've let sleeping dogs lie.

But out of love—love for his Savior, love for his church, indeed love for Maher—Colbert made a fool of himself on national television by giving a soliloquy just shy of a Billy Graham sermon to none other than Bill Maher. Knowing that everyone thought he was wrong, perhaps evil, and certainly a fool, he spoke out of love.

Are Colbert and Maher opposites? In some ways. Yet, they're also of a similar, rare ilk. In an age dominated by relativism, they are two men with the gumption and conviction to try and convert one another. The exchange should be studied by a church which finds herself in a similarly awkward, tense cultural moment.

Now, more than ever, we need to be reminded that the motivation of our faith is still love, and the content of our faith is still "foolishness to the Greeks." May we not resolve the cultural tension by changing the subject in the name of peace. Rather, may we invite all those who scorn and laugh at us into Christ's banquet hall. In other words, may we learn from Stephen Colbert how to be better, more loving fools.

12

THE CASE FOR THE CASE FOR CHRIST

I n 1981, a reporter for the Chicago Tribune converted from atheism to Christianity after exploring the evidence surrounding Jesus's death and resurrection. That reporter's story has sold some 14 million books and is now the subject of the newly released movie The Case for Christ.

Those familiar with Lee Strobel's journey and subsequent work in apologetics and theology won't be surprised by the content of the movie—which stays close to Strobel's account—but they may be surprised by the quality of the film's production, which leaps ahead of the recent pack of faith-based films. In addition to the stellar performances by Mike Vogel and Erika Christensen, the real-to-life set design capturing 1980s Chicago, and the well-pitched soundtrack, two themes make The Case for Christ a worthwhile movie.

More Than Experience

First, faith is more than an experience. While the movie is based on a true story, the narrative ultimately grounds itself in something larger than one man's experience with God. The point of the film isn't that God is "living on the inside." The point is that Jesus is living on the outside—risen from the dead, ruling at the right hand of the Father. If God isn't real on the outside (objectively), then Strobel doesn't want him on the inside (subjectively). He doesn't want "religious truth"; he wants true truth.

As he begins his investigation, a colleague at the Tribune tells him that the resurrection is the central tenet of the faith. If he can prove that this one event didn't happen, "the whole house of cards falls." From there, the film follows Strobel from one expert to another in his quest to "solve" the mystery of the resurrection.

Could the resurrection be a late invention? He consults an archeologist-turned-priest. Could it be a hoax? He has coffee with a biblical scholar. Could it be a mass hallucination? He visits the classroom of a famous agnostic psychologist. Could Jesus have survived the crucifixion? A world-renowned physician weighs in.

At one point, in a conversation with an atheist friend and father figure, Strobel realizes that his option isn't between faith and no faith; it's between well-grounded faith and foolish faith. His atheism requires more and more suspension of reason–and, to his surprise, the resurrection is more than the religious dogma he first thought; it's a reality, a fact with which to be reckoned.

More Than Reason

But that's not all. The film also makes clear that faith is more than reason. Strobel says early on in the movie that he only believes in what he can hear, see, smell, or touch. As a journalist, if he's going to believe in Christ, he'll need cold, hard evidence. I tend to wince a bit at such detective-type approaches to faith. After going down such a path, one can easily assume the role of Judge/God, as C. S. Lewis points out so well:

The ancient man approached God (or even the gods) as the accused person approaches his judge. For the modern man, the roles are quite reversed. He is the judge: God is in the dock. He is quite a kindly judge; if God should have a reasonable defense for being the god who permits war, poverty, and disease, he is ready to listen to it. The trial may even end in God's acquittal. But the important thing is that man is on the bench and God is in the dock.

And yet, while the nature of the narrative lends itself to being the sort of modern-apologetic Lewis decries, the writers largely avoid this pitfall. The subplot—concerning a man who may or may not have shot a police officer—reveals that Strobel sees only what he wants to see. He isn't a neutral, unbiased actor in a cosmic play.

Likewise, I appreciated the prominent place the director gave prayer—particularly in Leslie Strobel, Lee's wife. It's clear in the movie that reason will only take Lee so far. He needs more than a changed perspective; he needs a renewed spirit, a new heart.

This has always been the case. If people who saw the resurrected Messiah can still doubt (Matt. 28:17), then to have faith one obviously needs more than unadorned reason.

Indeed, one needs supernatural intervention. Ezekiel 11:19 is mentioned in the movie more than once: "I will remove from them their heart of stone and give them a heart of flesh." Strobel's faith journey includes reason, to be sure, but it also transcends reason. He sets out to examine Christ's resurrection with his mind; he ends up having his own heart resurrected in the process.

In this vein, I do wish the writers took the additional step to show the chief obstacle to belief: sin (Rom. 1:18–19). While the reasoning behind Strobel's atheism is questioned in many ways (the psychiatrist posits a "father wound" theory of unbelief), the movie gives almost no attention to the necessity of repenting of sin in the conversion process. Indeed, if you're looking for a clear gospel presentation in the film, you'll leave disappointed.

That said, despite its scattered weaknesses, The Case for Christ does justice to the compelling story of one man's extraordinary journey to faith. Not only does it deliver from a production standpoint, it also offers a powerful message of faith, transformation, and grace.

13

SAME LOVE, DIFFERENT GOD:

A GAY ANTHEM

Since I first heard Macklemore's *Same Love* in 2012, I've had a strange resonance with its message. This is odd because I'm a Conservative-Christian. That is, I not only adhere to the historic creeds of the church, but I'm seeking ordination in a denomination which adds even more confessional standards to the bunch! Perhaps more to the point, I'm a Christian-Conservative. By my early twenties, I'd devoured the works of Christopher Dawson, William F. Buckley, and Russell Kirk. If I thought they'd come, I'd invite George Will and David Brooks to my birthday party.

With such an Alex P. Keaton-pedigree, how could I be drawn to the lyrics of a song which gives voice to the liberal cry for LGBTQ rights? Was I falling victim to the ol' snappy rhythm-stupid lyric trap? Well, after hearing the song almost weekly for two years now, I've come to realize that my affinity for the message is not in spite of the lyrics, but because of the lyrics.

In fact, I think the song can work as a sort of tract for

explaining the position of Christian-Conservatives and Conservative-Christians. At its heart, *Same Love* argues: (1) Our view of sexuality is influenced by the culture. (2) Our personal sexuality is influenced by our "innate" selves. (3) Our sexuality is accountable to the one, true God.

First, our view of sexuality is influenced by the culture. At the beginning of the song, we're given a story.

"When I was in the 3rd grade I thought that I was gay 'cause I could draw,
> My uncle was and I kept my room straight
> I told my mom, tears rushing down my face, she's like,
> "Ben you've loved girls since before pre-K"
> Trippin', yeah, I guess she had a point, didn't she?
> A bunch of stereotypes all in my head
> I remember doing the math like "Yeah, I'm good a little league"
> A pre-conceived idea of what it all meant
> For those who like the same sex had the characteristics"

MACKLEMORE THOUGHT he was gay because he had certain characteristics generally thought of as "feminine." Thankfully, he had a thoughtful mother who told him that his sexuality is deeper than just his interests and sensibilities. In this regard, the church could learn a lot from Macklemore's mom. Let me tell you a story not dissimilar to the one Macklemore recounts. This one, an amalgamation of the stories of a number of my gay friends who were raised in conservative, evangelical churches, only to leave the faith for a gay lifestyle:

With my friends from school, I was reading Dostoevsky, playing Mozart, and reciting Shakespeare. At youth group, I was playing ultimate cow-tongue Frisbee, Call of Duty, and sitting through services which reminded me of a pep rally. Because of my "weird" sensibilities, I was called gay by my church before I was ever accepted as a gay man by the community with which I now identify. At first, I didn't think of myself as a homosexual; I just knew I wasn't straight by my church's standards. Two communities–two options–were before me; church community or gay community. Both groups told me that I had the sensibilities of the second group. So, eventually, I believed them both. Subsequently, I was embraced, nurtured, and freed by a loving community of gay friends at school.

PERHAPS OUR SHARPEST, most gifted church members left the faith because their church didn't have the theological or liturgical tools to show them how the creation and preservation of art fits into the redemptive schema of God. Sure, as Christians, there are certain character-qualities that should typify the life of a man or woman. These qualities complement the qualities of the opposite sex. However, there are numerous sensibilities and personality traits which must not be viewed as statically masculine or feminine.

One of the reasons it's so easy to create theories in which a figure from the past (like Abraham Lincoln) is gay, is because the traits typical of masculinity and femininity are constantly in flux. In Lincoln's day, to have a public display of emotion was more acceptable of a man than a woman. Obviously, in Ronald Reagan's day, that had changed.

Thus, a modern reader can anachronistically infer something about a 18th or 19th century man's sexual orientation from his "feminine" traits. Like Macklemore's mom, the church needs to recover a healthy, biblical doctrine of masculinity and femininity-a doctrine which avoids stereotypes and accounts for the artist and the athlete.

Second, our personal sexuality is influenced by our "innate" selves. Now, we've seen that cultural views of masculinity and femininity have something to do with how we view "gay" and "straight," and thus influence how we judge our own sexuality. However, that is not the whole story. The song goes on to say that we can't allow these cultural stereotypes to influence our personal sexuality.

> You [can't] be cured with some treatment and religion
>> Man-made, rewiring of a pre-disposition
>> Playing God

TO CHANGE your sexual identity is like playing God. You can't just go through a procedure to "fix" your orientation. It is innate to you. Now, a tension is set up in the song. On the one hand, we're born with physicality, with bodies. On the other hand, the song suggests, just because one is born with female genitalia, does not mean that one *is* female. One may be born female, but, in fact, be male. Here, the song prioritizes the metaphysical over the physical. What you feel is innate and right. What you are physically is subjective and possibly wrong.

Here is the tension: that which is "innate" is sometimes *physical* and other times *metaphysical*. When it is the feeling of hate (which the song mentions), it is wrong and should be changed. When it is the feeling of attraction toward someone of the same sex, it should be embraced. When the physicality is your gender, it can be amended.

When the physicality is your race (which the song mentions), it must be embraced and accepted. The song is right, you can't play God; you have to submit to your innate self. The question, however, is how do we know what is innate? Asked differently: "should I 'play god' and deny my feeling of same sex attraction?" or "Should I 'play god' and have a sex change?" You see, the decision isn't as easy as "to be myself or not?" No, the issue is "what part of myself will I 'not be?'"

This brings us to our third area of agreement with the song; our sexuality is accountable to the one, true God.

> Whatever God you believe in
>> We come from the same one
>> Strip away the fear
>> Underneath it's all the same love

THE SONG IS NOT PROMOTING a squishy relativism. It doesn't say "whatever god you believe in, it doesn't matter." Nor does it say, "Whatever god you believe in is true." No, you may (subjectively) believe in the Muslim god, or the Wiccan god, or the Buddhist god, but actually there is only one (objective) god.

Of course, having a god speak to us is the only way to resolve the tension of what is "innate" and "non-innate" to our humanity. To say something is innate is to say it can exist apart from brokenness and sin. The metal of a ship is innate, the rust is not.

Our age is made up of only broken things, so the only way to know what is innate is to know what existed before there was brokenness, and what will exist when the brokenness is taken away. Someone who knows the Alpha and the Omega has to tell us what is innate. Given our "situatedness" in history, we can't know such things on our own. Our sexuality can't be "discovered," it has to be given to us by our Creator.

Well, who is this one, true God? Macklemore claims to know him; indeed, he speaks for him. He lets us know that this god deems race (physical) and sexual preference (metaphysical) as innate; but judges hate (metaphysical) and gender (physical) as non-innate.

Macklemore doesn't think you should put your trust in a book "written 3,000 years ago." I get that. However, what's the alternative? Macklemore's told us that there is only one god, but what's this god's name? How did he and Macklemore meet? Macklemore is telling us what is innate and what is extraneous, what is good and what is bad, what is clean and what is unclean, what is holy and what is profane. Are we supposed to take his word for it that this is god's opinion?

While I agree that there is only one, true God, I think He is Yahweh; the one in whom Abraham put his trust, the one who Moses encountered in a cloud, the one who Paul knew, the one from whom Jesus claimed to be. Not only are other "gods" subject to Him (including Macklemore's god), but I am subject to him. My sexual orientation, gender, and proclivities are subject to him. You see, we can't base our sexual identity on the culture's view of masculinity and femininity, it's relative and ever fluctuating.

We can't base our sexual identity on our own impulses.

How would we know which are innate and which are bad? How would we know which to neglect and which to embrace? No, we have to base our sexual identity and practices on the one, true God. He created our gendered-bodies, and he has a plan for them stretching beyond this short life.

As a straight man, I resonate with *Same Love* because, in a sexually "open" and "evolving" world, I need a sure and steady word from God just as much as my gay friends do. Macklemore claims to have such a word. In fact, Jesus and Macklemore are making the exact same claim; both claim they know the will of the one, true God. Here is your choice: put your faith in the one who rose from the dead, or put your faith in the one who wrote *Thrift Shop*.

14

ART PREPARES US FOR SUFFERING

Theology is the North Pole and art the South Pole of the
Christian Life. Theology is the study of what God does and
says; art is what people say and do in the entire context of what
God says and does...You can't have one without the other."–
Eugene Peterson

THE PROBLEM of evil has long been a challenge to Christians—
how could an all loving, all powerful God allow pain and
suffering in his good creation? The question never remains
theoretical, of course. In one way or another, the problem will
pose itself to each us of directly. The question is, will we be
ready when we get the inevitable phone call that will bring us
to our knees? What can we do today to ready ourselves for the
heartache and pain of tomorrow? It may be counterintuitive,
but my answer is *go to an art gallery*.

The arts have always been a key means of spiritual formation and renewal in the church. Art beckons us to look higher, to look deeper—to recognize the transcendent in items as ordinary as canvas and clay. This transcendent experience poses its own dilemma that is a sort of counterpoint to the dilemma of evil.

Just as evil causes us to ask, "How could this exist if there's a God?" the goodness and order we see in art causes us to ask, "How could this exist if there isn't a God?" Indeed, we'll only be able to make sense of the world's ugliness in moments of crisis if we first try to make sense of the world's beauty in moments of transcendent joy. Dealing with the problem of pleasure will prepare us for the problem of pain.

Seeing Beyond

The great conductor and composer Leonard Bernstein put it beautifully:

> Beethoven turned out pieces of breathtaking rightness. Rightness—that's the word! Our boy has the real goods, the stuff from Heaven, the power to make you feel at the finish: something is right in the world. There is something that checks throughout, that follows its own law consistently: something we can trust, that will never let us down.

IN THE CHRISTIAN account of the world, creation is sacramental: it points beyond itself. But if we haven't trained our eyes to look for order and meaning in the symphony, we won't be likely to see with eyes of faith in the midst of tragedy. So, be it a piece of music, a painting, a sculpture—all art should lead our eyes beyond the immediate and to the infinite, beyond the creation itself to the Creator himself.

THIS IS a point C.S. Lewis makes in *The Weight of Glory*:

> The books or the music in which we thought the beauty was located will betray us if we trust to them; it was not in them, it only came through them, and what came through them was longing. These things—the beauty, the memory of our own past—are good images of what we really desire; but if they are mistaken for the thing itself they turn into dumb idols, breaking the hearts of their worshipers. For they are not the thing itself; they are only the scent of a flower we have not found, the echo of a tune we have not heard, news from a country we have never yet visited.

In the secular, de-mythologized West, our eyes are taught to look at and in, but never through, and certainly not up. Whatever you call this cultural phenomenon—objectivism, scientism, utilitarianism—its effects are palpable: we're habituated to see *creation* as *nature*, an end in itself, an object for our dissection but certainly not our delight.

In such a culture, appreciating art takes more discipline and effort than ever before. At first, the clay appears to be just that: a lump of dirt. Yet, if you make it your practice to stop by the same sculpture every time you visit the museum, over the months and years you will find that the clay transforms into something different entirely. It takes on new meaning and significance. But of course it is not the object itself that changes —it's how we see it. The seeing is changed not by the *seen* but by the *see-er*.

The thing is, *seeing* well takes intentionality, especially in our distracted age. To see more than a lump of dirt in a sculpture takes a patience that is rarer and rarer in our fast-paced age. But if we as Christ-followers want to honor God's beautiful creation (including the creations of his image-bearers), we need to cultivate this patient mode of seeing.

Problems of Pain and Pleasure

The conditions that make art appreciation difficult are the same conditions that make reckoning with the problem of evil difficult. The same eyes that see only a lump of clay in a sculpture will only see discoloration and scars when looking in the mirror after a major surgery. Conversely, the same eyes that are trained to see meaning and beauty while sitting on the bench at the museum will be able to recognize the handiwork of God while laying in the hospital bed, even as they yet see through a glass, dimly.

This is not to say we will *always* discover meaning just by looking at something hard enough. Meaning in art, as in suffering, is sometimes elusive or even inaccessible. The death of a loved one or relentless hardship can often feel senseless and devoid of meaning. Some overly artsy music or films can feel the same way. But the extremes do not detract from the broader principle. The more we cultivate intentional, observant viewing of art, the more we'll be able to make meaning of all of reality.

The arts are crucial in recovering the skills necessary to regain a right disposition toward reality. They can help us see order and cohesion in the true, the good, and the beautiful. Not only can a deep familiarity with the beautiful give us the standard by which we recognize and name the ugly, but once we've become accustomed to looking for meaning in moments of joy, perhaps we can also see with eyes of faith in moments of despair.

We might say it this way: The problem of pain becomes more manageable if we've already reckoned with the problem of pleasure.

15

A CLASSIC MOVIE MARTIN LUTHER WOULD LOVE

"I just had to try. . . . If we don't try, we don't do. And if we don't do, why are we here on this earth?" In the classic Civil War drama *Shenandoah* (1965), Mr. Anderson (Jimmy Stewart) asks this question following a failed attempt to rescue his son, taken prisoner by the Union Army after being mistaken as a Confederate soldier. When he returns home from the voyage, he takes count of his losses: half his children are now dead as a result of the rescue effort. If you've seen the movie, you know this is exactly what he was trying to avoid. It's why he wouldn't let any of his sons enlist in the war.

By the last scene, Mr. Anderson and the audience alike will understand the helpless state in which humans flounder. If we're to find a bulwark, a fortress in this life, we'll have to look outside ourselves. Indeed, the film ultimately concurs with Fleming Rutledge: "The message of Jesus Christ, in sum, is this: Salvation is not in your hands."

Vanity of Vanities

Protecting his children is Mr. Anderson's sole mission in life. Before his wife's death some 16 years earlier, Anderson apparently promised her as much. He also promised, at her request, to raise the children with faith—something he does only begrudgingly, as evidenced by the prayer he offers before dinner early in the film:

"LORD, we cleared this land. We plowed it, sowed it, and harvested. We cook the harvest. It wouldn't be here and we wouldn't be eating it if we hadn't done it all ourselves. We worked dog-bone hard for every crumb and morsel, but we thank you Lord just the same for the food we're about to eat. Amen."

AFTER COMING HOME, what's left of the family returns to the dinner table with a cloud of grief surrounding them. Mr. Anderson tries to pray his usual prayer, the one that accentuates his own efforts and minimizes God's, but he can't make it through. He shakes his head and stumbles out of the house and down to his wife's grave:

"I DON'T EVEN KNOW what to say to you any more, Martha. There's not much I can tell you about this war. It's like all wars, I guess. The undertakers are winning. And the politicians who talk about the glory of it. And the old men who talk about the need of it. And the soldiers, well, they just want to go home."

· · ·

AT THE GRAVE, Mr. Anderson realizes the futility of all human effort, not just his own. For all his striving, for all his work, for all the work of the politicians and old men, all is still lost. Vanity of vanities, all is vanity.

Our Striving Would Be Losing

Standing graveside, Anderson says: "I wish. . . I wish I could just know what you're thinking about it all, Martha. And maybe it wouldn't seem so bad to me if I knew what you thought about it. Just then, the church bells ring. "You never give up, do you?" Anderson says.

He makes his way back up to the house, rounds up the family, and goes to the church he's reluctantly attended for the past 16 years. As he walks in, "A Mighty Fortress Is Our God" is being sung. Anderson sits as an embodiment of Luther's words: *Did we in our own strength confide, our striving would be losing.*

Anderson confided in himself, and he lost everything. He plowed the field, but there was no harvest. Yet there is hope in his eyes. Having experienced the "striving would be losing" reality of confiding in himself, he now believes the lyric that follows:

"*Were not the right Man on our side, the Man of God's own choosing: Dost ask who that may be? Christ Jesus, it is he; Lord Sabaoth his name, from age to age the same, and he must win the battle.*"

As the song concludes, the long lost son—"Boy"—limps into the church. Tears well up in Anderson's eyes. At this moment—at his weakest, at his most vulnerable, when he's finally not confiding in his own strength—he experiences restoration. His wholeness is a gift from Lord Sabaoth, the God of Rest. With his arm around his son, Mr. Anderson sings the Doxology:

> *Praise God, from whom all blessings flow;*
> *Praise him, all creatures here below;*
> *Praise him above, ye heav'nly host;*
> *Praise Father, Son, and Holy Ghost*

Life of Thanks

Shenandoah is about many things—the ethics of war, family, the role of the citizen to the state—but chiefly it's about one question: Why are we on this planet? By the final scene, the film portrays a decidedly Christian answer: the true life is the eucharistic life, the life of thanks.

Indeed, I like to picture the Andersons after the church service, back at the table for Sunday lunch. In lieu of his typical prayer, perhaps Anderson dusts off a copy of one of Martha's books—one by Luther would seem appropriate after singing "A Mighty Fortress"—and he'd read to the family the following passage:

We cannot give God anything; for everything is already His, and all we have comes from Him. We can only give Him praise, thanks, and honor.

Then, he and his family would do just that.

16

THE MAGIC OF THE MAGIC SCHOOL BUS

Change is hard—like, super hard. That's the theme of the first episode of Netflix's *The Magic School Bus Rides Again*. The episode was a diatribe aimed squarely at those of us who grew up reading the books and watching the original cartoon. It's true; the show is different—new storylines, a new Ms. Frizzle (gasp!), and digital animation rather than the classic 2D. But if we 90's kids can get past the cosmetic differences, we'll find that the charm of *The Magic School Bus* remains. The genius of the franchise has never been in the things Netflix changed, but in what they kept: the way in which Ms. Frizzle and her class approach science.

Though the school bus is able to transport the kids across space and time, the students are never more amazed at the magic of the bus than at the complexity and order of the world. Far from distracting the students, the bus's magic only aids the class in their pursuit of truth. By, say, shrinking into a raindrop, they're not only able to know *about* environmental science, they're able, in some sense, to *know* environmental science personally. The class never remains distant or removed from the world. Rather, they lovingly enter into the episode's subject, literally encountering the world from the inside.

Contrast this disposition toward the world with that of another Netflix reboot, *Bill Nye Saves the World*. Nye doesn't enter into a cloud to appreciate the beauty of a thunderstorm; rather, he places H_2O in beakers and under a microscope. For Nye, science is not about marveling at matter, it's about mastering it. At best, Nye sees the universe as a complex code, but even then his job is to crack it, not revel in its complexity.

Playing the consummate Modern scientist, Nye is always a step removed from his study—observing and experimenting from above, goggles firmly secured. Typically, he doesn't go out into the habitat of the object he's inspecting, he instead brings the thing into his environment. Rather than entering a garden to study a flower, he cuts the flower open in his lab, seeking to understand the flower's totality by dissecting its parts. If Ms. Frizzle learns by joining in a thing's life, then Nye learns by taking the thing's life.

In his wonderful book *The Relevance of Physics*, Stanley L. Jaki shows how Modernity "depersonalized" science in such a way. Before one can do science, one must stand aback from the world, obtaining a state of neutral objectivity. The coldness of our study is necessitated by the chillness of our subject; namely, nature. Says Jaki,

"IT WAS as if one were to consider the beautiful display on the stage of nature a poetic disguise and look for the ultimate reality in the ugly, soulless mesh of ropes, pulleys, and levers found backstage."

. . .

TAKING Jaki's theatrical illustration further, our belief—or lack thereof—in a divine Director influences our view of the play (i.e. nature), and the play can likewise lead us to a deeper understanding of the Director. Theologians have long recognized this mutually conversant relationship between "general" and "special" revelation.

Tertullian captures the dynamism well, "God first sent forth nature as a teacher, intending also to send prophecy next, so that you, a disciple of nature, might more easily believe prophecy." Unfortunately, Christians often listen to this dialog with one ear; sensitive to the ways nature can inform our theology, but deaf to the ways in which our theology informs our view of nature.

Again, Jaki's analogy is helpful: If there is no Director, then the galaxy we've happened upon is simply an incident—full of drama, no doubt, but as devoid of structure as it is of a script. What we see historically is that our method of scientific inquiry became depersonalized at exactly the same time as our view of the universe became depersonalized. If there is no Director, there is no play; if there is no play, we cease leaning into the movements of the world as *interpreters* and instead adopt the reclining posture of *observers*.

Thus, using the langue of educational theorist Parker J. Palmer, Bill Nye the Modern Guy (Bill! Bill! Bill!) approaches the world with curiosity and control, but not love. Love for the object one is studying personally bonds the subject (the scientist) with his subject (science). The Modernist will lament, "Such subjectivity has no place here!"

The presence of "subjectivity," however, is only a negative in science if it is always a hindrance to discovery. Palmer, for one, doesn't see the presence of subjectivity as wrong precisely because love can only occur when the subject is included, and love is necessary to fully know a given thing. Palmer clarifies:

"No scientist knows the world merely by holding it at arm's length: if we ever managed to build the objectivist wall between the knower and the known, we could know nothing except the wall itself. Science requires an engagement with the world, a live encounter between the knower and the known. That encounter has moments of distance, but it would not be an encounter without moments of intimacy as well."

If curiosity and control create distance from the world, love intertwines the knower with the known in what Palmer elsewhere calls the "web" or "connective tissue" of reality. Such a loving disposition toward science can only be implemented if reality is in fact a web, if connective tissue between the whole of creation actually exists. Were the world disparate and random, love would indeed only get in the way of our study. However, if creation is cohesive, purposeful—dare I say *designed*—then we know it most truly when we're receiving its message with love, awe, and gratitude.

This is not to say Nye is never amazed at nature—he surely is. But the anti-modern method of inquiry practiced in *The Magic School Bus* tempts one to move beyond amazement to *thankfulness*. At the end of each episode, after the students have gained a new insight, there is a kinetic, indescribable energy in the classroom. It almost reaches articulation when the students —full of wonder at the world—thank Ms. Frizzle for their experience.

But even this moment, in all its earnest beauty, doesn't do justice to the class' seeming reverence. No doubt they're thankful *for* Ms. Frizzle, as they are thankful *for* the world that they now understand at a deeper level, but *to whom* are they thankful? Philosopher David McPherson is correct in saying:

"What we need—as reflective, meaning-seeking beings—is an ontology that can make sense of the phenomenology, where the phenomenology is justified to be a fitting response to the way the world is (viz. its sacred or reverence-worthy character)."

While *The Magic School Bus* never transports the class into the incorporeal realm to answer that ontological question, the way in which Ms. Frizzle approaches the world is nevertheless undergirded by a particular metaphysic—one hostile to the materialistic scientism of Bill Nye. Nye approaches the world as *chaos*; Ms. Frizzle approaches the world as *cosmos*. Ms. Frizzle's pedagogy depends upon the "inner truth" of all things, in Augustinian parlance.

This peculiar posture toward science allows Ms. Frizzle to lead her students to a deeper sort of learning than the kind offered by Nye. Rather than preforming various experiments upon *nature*, Ms. Frizzle facilitates experiences within *creation*. Thanks to Netflix, we can once again buckle up and take a seat in her classroom, experiencing anew the magic found in an old school bus, if not in the world itself.

17

MOVING THE MODERN MIND

Does modern education make people less likely to have their minds changed by sound arguments? That's Tejenig Topjian's claim in the aptly titled article *Why Education and Philosophy Stand in Opposition to Each Other*. Debating metaphysical truth-claims has fallen out of fashion lately. Philosophy is no longer able to persuade because our educational system is geared toward "indoctrinating kids about specific facts and theories" rather than teaching the larger "process of knowledge creation, information processing, truth seeking, and critical evaluation."

In other words, the modernly educated lack the critical-thinking skills necessary to properly evaluate various perspectives. So we don't engage new ways of thinking with an open mind; we dig in our heels, relying on what we already know. What we lack in smarts, oddly, we make up for in stubbornness.

Elizabeth Kolbert shows how this works in a recent New Yorker article, "Why Facts Don't Change Our Minds." After recounting a number of studies on how "first impressions" are extremely immalleable in the face of new, challenging evidence, Kolbert identifies what she calls a "myside bias." Essentially, this means humans "aren't randomly credulous. Presented with someone else's argument, we're quite adept at spotting the weaknesses. Almost invariably, the positions we're blind about are our own."

By not teaching students how to think critically, modern education only reinforces this "myside bias." In the end, there's only one path forward for Topjian:

> The only way the above two ideas wouldn't contradict each other is if our education system was in fact built to teach thinking. If we were teaching kids how to think and not what to think, then when they are exposed to new ideas and conflicting information, they will have the mental tools to discern good ideas from bad ones.

As an educator, I'm sympathetic to this argument. Education writ large has abandoned the liberating arts for a more pragmatic, technical sort of schooling. While the education of yesteryear was focused on forming the right sort of person—one able to think for himself or herself—modern education is geared toward training the right sort of professional, one bound to a trade.

This is why C. S. Lewis goes so far as to call liberal learning "for freemen" and vocational training "for slaves." The former frees the students to navigate truth on their own (thus flourish), while the later simply teaches them to use the tools in front of them (thus function). The former is focused on who the student *is* while the later emphasizes what the student *does*.

The net result of this educational shift is that philosophy, logic, and the like find little traction among the modernly educated. They know *what* they know, but they lack the old tools once used to know *how* to know. The McDonaldization of education is skilled at giving out fish sandwiches to the masses, but is ill equipped to teach individual pupils how to fish, let alone how to use the deep fryer.

As a Christian, however, I'm not quite ready to give up on our culture. In fact, I would say we uniquely have the tools necessary to answer Topjian's lament-filled question: "If it takes two decades to teach people how the world works, how is a portion of that learning supposed to be undone in just a few hours of reading or argumentation?"

While our current climate may make the "undoing of learning" through philosophizing difficult, it doesn't mean persuasion is a hopeless enterprise altogether. After all, humans are complex; no one is a brain on a stick. Even if we can't appeal to the head, we can still persuade the hands and the heart.

Persuading the hands

Topjian says modern education is concerned with "teaching young people how the world is." Modern education is tactile, appealing to the practical, the pragmatic. Christians shouldn't view such a background as a particularly unusual stumbling block. Too often, we've bought into the modern lie that reality is "secular" or "neutral." Insofar as we see "street smarts" as somehow incompatible with biblical wisdom, we're leaning more on Gnosticism than Christianity.

This world is in fact *creation*; that is, it has a Creator, God.

All that exists is His—even reality. Epistemologist Esther Lightcap Meek puts it beautifully, "Creation is the outcome of a divine conversation, 'let there be!' Reality is thus an epiphany—a word of God's steadfast love."

So that wisdom gained from bumping up against reality is heavenly wisdom; and that wisdom learned from Scripture is practical wisdom. If someone isn't immediately drawn to a theological discussion, we must not lose hope! They are walking on God's territory if they're fixing a bike, writing code, or organizing a business, not just when they're thinking through the problem of evil. We must become more skilled at appealing to the concrete logic of the hands. Moving from the practical/tactile to the theoretical/metaphysical is a persuasive, biblical apologetic move. Ask Solomon.

Persuading the heart

At the end of the day, the main stumbling block preventing one from being persuaded by the gospel is not intellectual anyhow. According to St. Paul, we suppress the truth of God for a lie, exchanging the invisible for the visible. Our brains are not idiotic, our hearts are idolatrous. If we come to see evangelistic encounters in this way—spiritual struggles of the heart rather than intellectual sparring matches—we'll come to see the modernly educated as no different than any other human: bursting with dignity, yet broken and in need of a heart transformation. Of course, this doesn't exclude philosophical augment, etc. but neither does it depend on such tactics. I've always been fascinated by C. S. Lewis' description of his conversion:

I was driven to Whipsnade one sunny morning. When we set out I did not believe that Jesus Christ is the Son of God, and when we reached the zoo I did. Yet I had not exactly spent the journey in thought. Nor in great emotion. It was more like when a man, after a long sleep, still lying motionless in bed, becomes aware that he is now awake.

IN THE END, I'm discouraged by the lack of critical thought and philosophical inquiry in our cultural moment. There is a real need to shift education back to its liberal roots. However, I have hope that persuasion is still possible precisely because the gospel isn't about a philosophy, it's about a Person; and it's not an argument, it's an announcement.

Lewis' description of his experience is heartening as we seek to persuade seemingly unmovable minds. The Gospel is divine smelling salts—able to awake the hands, heart, and even the head from the deepest of slumbers.

18

INTELLECTUAL CURRENCY

As I write, there is a nip in the air—autumn is just around the corner. Indeed, next week, colleges across the country will commence their Fall semester. Many students who grew up in Christian homes will consciously trade in their faith for a philosophical system antithetical to the one of their upbringing. Even more students, however, while not outright denying their Christian faith, will unconsciously adopt a philosophical system that is inherently idolatrous.

It's not that this second group wants to be idolaters; they simply lack the tools to discern the nature of the bill of goods their professor is selling them. So, how can one know if a given philosophical system (Kantianism, Marxism, Platonism, etc.) is idolatrous?

One can begin by asking two questions. First, "is this logical?" Second, "is this sinful?" If the answer is "yes" to the first question, the answer will be "no" to the second question. If the answer is "no" to the first question, the answer will be "yes" to the second question.

Here's a story to illustrate the point: On her twenty first birthday, Cindy was promised a night on the town with her girl-friends. After dinner, her friends came to her house in a limo, blindfolded her, and took her to *Crazy Dave's Casino* (obviously, she had some pretty lame friends...). As they were getting into the limo, they shoved some bills in her purse and said "tonight's on us!" Once inside, Cindy took off her blindfold. Because there was no signage on the inside of the building, Cindy still wasn't sure where she was.

Eventually, she saw a waitress and asked if she could get something to drink. As she pulled out her wallet to pay, she saw four hundred *Crazy Dave's Casino-Bucks* in her purse.

Now, there are only two ways that Cindy could have deduced her location. First, she could have spotted a logo. While it's true the big *Crazy Dave's* sign was outside, there were actually logo's on the slot machines, napkins, etc.

Secondly, of course, she could've known by looking at the *Crazy Dave's Casino-Bucks*. Her currency could've revealed to her the location. Likewise, her location could have told her what sort of currency her friends slipped into her purse. For Cindy to answer the question "am I at *Casino Dave's?*" she'd have to look at her currency. For her to answer the question "what sort of currency do I have in my purse?" she'd have to look at the signage. Back to our original question: how can one know if a given philosophical system is idolatrous? There are at least two ways:

Firstly, you can look for signage. Here, you're trying to deter-mine if the system ostensibly advertises itself as sinful. Put simply, this means asking a couple questions of the philosoph-ical system.

One question is, "does it enable me to do something God forbids?" Nihilism, for instance, enables one to tear down systems for "tearing's" sake. Well, some systems need to be torn down, but we're commanded to obey God's rule. Any tearing, then, must not be for its own sake, but because we're seeking a system patterned after the rule of God. Thus, we know Nihilism is idolatrous because it enables us to do something God forbids.

Another question to ask is, "does the system forbid me from doing something God commands?" Animism, for instance, is idolatrous because it teaches that everything on the earth, indeed the earth itself, has a soul. Thus, I'm forbidden from, among other things, giving thanks to God. If "Mother Nature" is giving me food, my thanksgiving is directed to the object I'm eating rather than the One who gave me the object to eat. Like Cindy, you're in a building (the *Casino of Idolatry*, if you will), and you're looking for clues as to the nature of the structure.

Secondly, you can look at the currency in which the philosophical system deals. This is crucial because not all philosophical systems are easily detected as "sinful." Like Cindy in the casino, there isn't a big *Crazy Dave's* sign, and the logos are quite small and inconspicuous. Thus, it won't do to simply ask "am I in the *Casino of Idolatry*?"

Rather, you'll have to ask "am I using the currency of the *Casino of Idolatry*?" Well, what is the currency of idolatry? In a word, it's illogicality. If the system is illogical, it is idolatrous. Idolatry is always making a deal in which you trade life for death; the family blessing for some soup. An idolatrous philosophical system never uses the currency of "logic." Thus, one can ask the question, "Are the propositions which this philosophy proposes logical?" If the answer is "no!" then you can know the system is itself idolatrous.

With a little deductive reasoning, one can find idolatry in

any illogical statement. Likewise, one can find incoherence in any given expression of idolatry. It's incumbent upon those of us responsible for educating tomorrows college students, then, to teach them how think Christianly, faithfully, logically.

19

TEACHING HISTORY THEOLOGICALLY

In class, I'm often asked if we'll be studying theology or history on that particular day. I know what the student means; a class on "historical theology" is vast—some days we'll look exclusively at Scripture, other days we'll focus in on, say, the Crusades. However, the question itself reveals a bias which all of us children of modernity share: the propensity to separate the "religious" from the "factual," "history" from "theology."

While theology and history can be distinguished, they can never be properly separated. It's my contention that history and theology share three things in common which exclude the possibility of hermitically sealing one from another.

First, theology and history share creation. One could define history as "the story of this world." At first blush, this definition seems to isolate "theology" from "history." However, the "the story of this world" is precisely that with which theology is concerned! History and theology are both concerned with the same substance: namely, creation. Both disciplines are concerned with telling the same story; namely, "the story of this world"

The Bible does not limit its sights to the "spiritual." Rather, the Bible mischievously puts its nose in families, mountains, lakes, kings, nations, and other historical, created things. In fact, when not speaking about God himself, the Bible speaks about nothing but creation, the very same creation with which history is out to chronicle! Theology and history are narrating the same epic. These are the cards Christians are dealt. Should one want a religion which tells the story of a different world, there's always the mystical, Eastern tables; but from Genesis to Revelation, the Bible is telling the true story of *this* world.

Second, theology and history share sin. When you put theology in a silo far from history, you lose the ability to call past events "wrong" or "right." For instance, nearly all historians will characterize the move from chattel slavery, to the Emancipation Proclamation, to the civil rights marches, as a positive progression. Even atheistic historians will want to call the freeing of slaves "good." But by what standard is it good?

Perhaps you think, "but the ideal historian will not take sides, he'll just state the facts." Hopefully, anyone who's watched the History Channel when *Pawn Stars* isn't on will recognize the naiveté of such a sentiment. Even in deciding which events to recall and which to leave out, the historian is constructing a narrative in which there are "good" and "bad" actors. In this instance, the atheist historian is assuming the moral presuppositions of Christianity.

Third, theology and history share salvation. Two thousand years ago Jesus came, in history, to liberate the fallen creation from sin. His physical corpse was then, in time and space, raised from the dead. For the theological category of "redemption" to be intelligible, history must be employed.

Indeed, for the resurrection to happen, a personal God would have to be tinkering around in history. The theological claim that Christ rose from the dead, like nearly every theological claim, is by nature a historical one (1 Cor 15). The "theological Jesus" claims to be historical and the "historical Jesus" claims to be "theological." If you separate the "theological" Jesus from the "historical" Jesus, you lose both.

In conclusion, teaching history theologically requires skill, but not the skill one might expect. The skill one must master is not that of deftly weaving together two, unrelated disciplines. Rather, it's a more passive, receptive skill. It's the skill of reading history and theology with the sensitivity to see their inherent connective tissue; the creational, moral, redemptive threads essential to both disciplines. Whether the Christian is teaching art, philosophy, science, or any other subject, he does so with the sure knowledge that this world is created and actively governed by a covenantal, Triune, personal God.

Thus, a distinctively Christian pedagogy tears down the artificial barriers between all "subjects." Christ's entire mission is one of unification: Heaven with earth, us with himself, us with the Father, us with one another, us with ourselves. How could education, then, be anything but a process of de-compartmentalization? First of subjects, then of our very person: Christ making our thoughts, desires, and actions coherent, whole, human. To the question, "are we studying history or theology today?" I now answer, "yes!

20

TEACHING THE BIBLE THEOLOGICALLY

When explaining a redemptive-historical approach to Scripture to those who've never been exposed to a "theological" or "typological" hermeneutic, I tend to spend most of my time emphasizing the Old Testament's use of itself, leaving questions of the New Testament's use of the Old for a later day.

There are several reasons for this, ranging from pragmatic (people tend to be less familiar with specific OT passages, and are thus more open to new readings), to temperamental (I personally have more fun in OT discussions than NT bull sessions), to pedagogical. In regards to what I perceive to be legitimate pedagogical reasons, there are at least three:

Firstly, I want people to be trained at the same hermeneutical boot-camp that the apostles attended. Peter and Paul were not "making it up as they went!" Rather, they were implementing the tools and skills which they learned from Jeremiah and Isaiah.

To be sure, the apostles had new revelation which significantly changed the "things" they saw, but they were "seeing" in a way congruent with preceding revelation. In other words, the flow of the Bible is set in Genesis; the rest of Scripture goes with that flow, even while adding greater specificity and nuance to the nature of God's redemptive plan.

If people are firmly grounded in the way, say, Micah interprets early revelation; they won't be as scandalized by the way in which John references the OT. Furthermore, they will feel free and equipped to read the Scriptures in an apostolic way. Said negatively, they won't feel as free or equipped to utilize a hermeneutic alien to the Scriptures.

Secondly, I want people to draw richer, more textured typological connections. Often, a theological reading of Scripture will only connect a given type with either (1) Eden/Adam, (2) Jesus, or (3) the Eschaton. Certainly, Protology, Christology, and Eschatology are the widest doors through which to enter the typological world of Scripture, but they're far from the only access-points.

For example, as the quote below will point out, David is not only a "new Adam" and a prefigurement of Christ, he's also a "new Moses," just as the temple is not only a "new creation" but also a "new tabernacle and alter." If you go straight to questions of the NT's use of the OT, you're likely to miss the canonical-complexity of a given type. However, if you're familiar with the types drawn in the OT, you'll see that the shadow of your substance also has a shadow; once both shadows are considered the substance becomes all the more substantive!

Lastly, I want people to see that the God of history is a poet, and the God of poetry is historic. This point is most easily shown through the creation account. Evangelical Interpreters generally line up on the side of "theological/literary" or "historical."

Theological folk tend to insist that the literary connections they see between the creation of the world and the temple, or other Ancient Near Eastern literature, make any historical claim about God's creative act invalid. Meanwhile, the historical folk are so busy asking the questions proposed by science and archeology that they never get around to asking literary questions of the literature.

The solution must not lie in a total rejection of both parties. Rather, the solution lies in a rejection of the bifurcation fallacy imbedded in the presuppositions of both arguments. The very historicity of the creation account is theological, just as its theological implications are historical. Once one begins reading the historical books of the Old Testament with eyes to see the typological connections throughout, one finds the insularity of the "historical" and "theological" parties intolerable.

The historical accounts recorded in Scripture invite the reader to make literary connections we typically associate with literary theory. Why? Because history isn't a random series of events. No, history is a beautiful, epic comedy being told by the great Poet-Redeemer.

Perhaps the easiest OT book in which to see these typological connections is Jonah, which I've written on here. However, what Jonah has in ease, Chronicles has in rich-complexity, as Scott Hahn shows in is magisterial commentary on 1 and 2 Chronicles:

"Like any good historian, the Chronicler provides a record of past figures, places, and events; but his accounting is written in such a way that these figures, places, and events often appear as types— signs, patterns, and precursors—intended to show his readers not

only the past but also their present reality from God's perspective. David is sketched as both a new Adam and a new Moses; the temple is a new creation and a new tabernacle and alter. In the Chronicler's account, the faithlessness and failures of Israel's first king, Saul, are replayed by kings centuries later. Saul is more than a failed monarch: he becomes the type of the unrighteous king who leads God's people to ruin and exile. In the same way, good kings in Chronicles do the things that David did—because David is a prototype of the righteous king.

Acknowledging this intensely inner-biblical and typological narrative technique is not to deny the historical reliability of the Chronicler's account. Rather, I am suggesting that reporting history 'as it happened' is not the Chronicler's sole interest. What happened in the past is crucial for the Chronicler, but only because in the what of history he sees the patterns of divine intention and intervention revealed—the why of history. The why of history is the reason for the Chronicler's work, which seeks not only to document past events but also to interpret these events in light of his readers' present needs for guidance and hope in the face of an uncertain future.

The way the Chronicler comes to understand, interpret, and explain the why of salvation history is through typology. As an intensely typological work, Chronicles gives us a typological interpretation of history (Hahn 2005c: 19-25). Typology for the Chronicler is a way to shed light on the unity of God's plan in history and to show the meaning of people, places, and events in light of God's covenant promises and redemptive acts. "

What the Chronicler is doing, which could be called "theological history," is the hermeneutical heartbeat of Scripture. While I'm uneasy with some of Scott Hahn's arguments in his self-described "Theological Commentary", I do think he does a remarkably good job of situating the Chronicler in his canonical context. What Hahn said above about Chronicles is equally applicable to most of the Old Testament. Indeed, if one spends adequate time considering the story, structure, and hermeneutic of the OT, the NT can be read for what it is: the climax of Israel's history.

21

THREE CHEERS FOR WORLDVIEW EDUCATION

To imagine oneself in the place of another is the only human future."-David Dark

UPTON SINCLAIR ONCE QUIPPED, "It is difficult to get a man to understand something when his salary depends upon his not understanding it." Rod Dreher—channeling a recent lecture by Joshua Gibbs—has outlined "the problem with worldview education." As one who gets a paycheck from providing such an education, I'm aware that I'm not approaching the issue from a neutral position. But heck, I'm a worldview teacher; I know there isn't such a creature as neutrality anyhow, so why not offer a brief defense?

To be clear, I wasn't at the conference to hear Joshua's lecture, so my critique is limited to a short article by Gibbs and Dreher's summation of his speech, which begins:

I agree

The problem with worldview education, [Gibbs] said, is that it closes off the possibility of wonder by providing a rigid ideological measuring stick for texts. Gibbs said it gives students unearned authority over a book. Hand them 'The Communist Manifesto,' they open it up, say, 'Marxist!', then case it aside. Hand them 'Thus Spake Zarathustra,' they open it up, see Nietzsche's name, say, 'Nihilist!' — and cast it aside.

Positively, I'm appreciative of the danger of "unearned authority" over a text. In my worldview class at least, we read Plato before discussing Platonism, we read Camus before discussing Existentialism. What I'm after is honesty—taking people at their word, not imposing an alien agenda onto them.

Good way to do things.

My decision to organize the curriculum as such has as much to do with pedagogy as it does integrity, however. It seems to me humans learn by approaching the world from the particular to the general. We don't learn the "principle of sowing and reaping" and then act accordingly. Rather, we do or don't study for a test and then do or don't receive a good grade. From those experiences, over time, we come to understand sowing and reaping at a conceptual level. Likewise, before one identifies an "ism" associated with a person, one must do the difficult, honest work of first reading the person.

Dreher goes on:

Gibbs was not arguing for Marxism on nihilism. He was saying that to truly encounter and wrestle with a great book (even a great bad book!), you have to enter into its world. For example — and this is me saying this, not him — in order to understand where Marxism comes from, you need to put yourself in the place of the man who hears something liberating in, 'Workers of the world, unite! You have nothing to lose but your chains.' Why did Marxism sound plausible and morally righteous to people once upon a time? What does it get right about justice? What does it get wrong? How do we know?

Here, it seems Dreher is arguing contra Gibbs. Gibbs, If I'm understanding him correctly, is saying students should read the words "workers of the world, unite!" nakedly, taking no note of any plausibility structure (i.e. worldview) which may make such words intelligible and attractive. Indeed, such context would only prevent wonder, according to Gibbs. Now, I'm with Dreher here—it is worthwhile indeed to enter the man's world, understand the given biases at play. When done well, such a worldview education doesn't cause the student to toss the book aside; far from it! It rather opens the book up anew to the student. Making the word "worldview" synonymous with "lazy/dismissive thinking" is, ironically, lazy and dismissive.

You see, worldview education begins with the humble premise that we aren't approaching the world "from above." As the poet Anne Carson put it, "There is no objective place." We are creatures, bound by space and time. We don't offer some supposed "neutral" interpretation of a given book, painting, data point, or fact. Rather, conscious or not of our myriad prejudices, we encounter the world *Christianly*. Likewise, every other reader, connoisseur, or scientist comes to the world from their own particular angle.

Worldview education seeks, imperfectly no doubt, to give these angles a voice at the Harkness table. Could such an education make students arrogant as Gibbs fears? I suppose. However, does the alternative make the student any less arrogant: supposing that the texts they are reading are composed by context-less men, and that they are encountering them

[handwritten margin note: I think so.]

unencumbered by their own commitments, values, and motives? I think not.

Gibbs problem with worldview, he's clarified, begins with the fact that it's too ethereal, unlike dogma:

> ...*the genuine problem I have with taking worldviews so seriously is that they are built on presuppositions, not dogma. Presuppositions exist in the world of ideals, the world of forms, however, dogma is composed and enforced by human beings.*

He illustrates the point thusly,

> *Men do not love ideas, but they will die for their wives. When I say I am conservative, I really mean that I believe everything Remi Brague and Edmund Burke say about history.* Ha!

So, worldview is concerned with "ideals," while dogma is in the human realm, "composed and enforced by human beings." Practically, this means, "A man may not claim to be Lutheran if he has not submitted himself to Lutheran authorities who have received his vow of loyalty to Lutheran dogma." To the Lutheran, Gibbs says, "be more Lutheran!"

While many Lutherans would laud Gibbs' advice to order the ecclesial over the ethereal, Martin Luther most certainly would not. For Luther, justification by faith alone in Christ alone is an ideal for which he'd die. Dogma merely composed and enforced by human beings be damned, Luther is hungry for more than ecclesial identification—he craves truth.

To be sure, Luther is happy to submit to human authority so long as it aligns with God's authority (found in Scripture), but not a minute longer. To go against conscience is neither safe nor right, after all. Even if, for the sake of argument, worldviews were as abstract as Gibbs claims, if the classroom isn't the place to discuss such ideas, where is?

More than Processing

Gibbs' chief problem with worldview analysis is that it smacks of an "enlightened" (i.e. modern) sensibility. It applies an inappropriate rubric to the medium, "That which is created in a state of wonder cannot be properly received in a spirit of efficiency and reason."

I certainly agree that one needs the right spirit with which to receive a given piece of art. However, I don't see how the Christian worldview is inherently antithetical to such a spirit of reception. If Gibbs does not want his students interpreting art Christianly, how does he want them interpreting?

Perhaps he'll say, "one need not analyze at all. Wonder at the art, don't interpret." To ask of the students this is to ask of them the impossible. Indeed, only a few paragraphs later, Gibbs says that Rhiana's music is "*about* the unconditional pursuit of personal pleasure."

If Gibbs, who is consciously trying to avoid "enlightened" sensibility, can't listen to a Rhiana song without doing a worldview analysis, how can he expect his students to read a whole book without being sullied by interpretation?

I say sullied ironically, of course. When sensitive to the worldviews at play, our reading and appreciation of art is only enhanced. Culture is religion externalized; to crack open, say, the ever-enchanting *Seven Voyages of Sinbad the Sailor* without considering Islamic thought is to "kiss your bride through a veil," as it were. This is as true of non-fiction as of fiction, biography as autobiography, painting as sculpture, dance as theater.

A Move to Story

Many of the issues I have with Gibbs complaints come down to category differences. I don't think it's all that helpful to categorize "worldview" as presupposition and "dogma" as supposition. One could implicitly presuppose a dogma, as the church did with the Trinity pre-Nicaea; and a worldview entails explicitly defined doctrines, like creation ex nihilo. Better, in my mind, is thinking of worldview as a narrative through which one makes sense of the world.

Once one thinks of a worldview as a story one comes to see "worldview analysis" as synonymous with "interpretation"—a necessity of our narratival nature. Indeed, there is no event, sentence, or fact too large or too small to escape the need for interpretation. NT Wright gives a wonderful example of how this works:

What is the meaning of the following comment? "It is going to rain." On the surface, the statement seems to be quite clear. Yet the meaning and significance of this remark can only be understood when we see the part it plays in a broader narrative. If we are about to go for a picnic that has been planned for some time, then these words would be bad news, with the further implication that perhaps we had better change our plans. If we live in East Africa plagued by drought, where another lengthy dry spell and consequent crop failure appears imminent, the statement would be good news indeed. If I had predicted three days ago that it would rain and you had not believed me, the statement would vindicate my predictive ability as a meteorologist. If we are part of the community of Israel on Mount Carmel listening to the words of Elijah, the statement substantiates the message of Elijah that Yahweh is the true God and that Elijah is his prophet. In each case, the single statement demands to be 'heard' within the context of a full implicit plot, a complete implicit narrative.

I'm confused

IF "IT IS GOING TO RAIN" can have such varied interpretations, how much more so birth, death, sex, art, love, and pain? I agree with Gibbs, an enlightened theory of man won't do. But I see such a theory as offering exactly what he offers: a set of dogmas, religious facts, no more—as if the student is a piece of hardware simply waiting on the teacher to download in him the correct software.

Conversely, a worldview education offers more than edicts, it offers what Scripture offers, an epoch. If Scripture is a myth grand enough to make sense of our enchanted cosmos, surely it's grand enough to make sense of Macbeth. As Gibbs showed, it can certainly make sense of Rhiana.

If I'm right in claiming that (1) everyone interprets narratively and (2) Scripture offers a grand story, then why insist that students not use the Scriptural story (i.e. Christian worldview) to interpret a given object? Further, how does better understanding the story in which an author lives (i.e. his worldview) hamper wonder in the reader? Insisting that a reading of a book without respect to the author's worldview produces more wonder is like insisting that puns are most amusing when the innuendo isn't caught. Worldview education isn't an obstacle to wonder, it's a vehicle to wonder.

In the end, having read countless articles by Gibbs over the years, I have no doubt that he and I share common educational

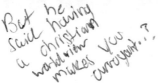
But he said having a christian worldview makes you arrogant...?

philosophies and goals. Further, his fear of creating thoughtless readers is valid. I also see too many students quite willing to dismiss foreign ideas out of hand. However, training students in worldviews—teaching students the empathetic skills needed to see the world through another's eyes—is not the problem. Indeed, worldview education is the solution.

22

STUDENT ANXIETY: THE NAKED TRUTH

"I felt naked." Those were the words of one student after leading her classmates in a discussion on the previous day's reading. "My dad told me if I get nervous talking in front of others, I should picture everyone else naked. That didn't work. I was the one exposed, not them." While she was prepared, engaged, and articulate, she nevertheless came up short in her own eyes. She's not alone.

For many, the anxiety felt during Socratic seminars not only prevents them from enjoying the conversation; pedagogically, they're prevented from comprehending or retaining any of the lively discussion. She ended our conversation with a phrase I've heard time and again, "I just can't express myself in front of others."

That last sentiment—about self-expression—helped place her initial feeling of nakedness in context. Understanding and addressing this dynamic has greatly increased my ability to help every student engage more freely in class discussions, not just the gregarious few. Once one understands that entering class discussions with the goal of self-expression actually hinders their ability to communicate, they're able to converse in a more loving, humane way. To understand how to achieve such a classroom culture, we have to understand nakedness.

Interestingly, Adam and Eve don't become naked as a result of their sin, they become aware of their nakedness as a result of their sin. More than shame, they become hyper self-aware. They become awkwardly, painfully self-conscious. They look to themselves after they sinned precisely because they looked to themselves when they sinned.

While they were called to look wholly to God for direction, provision, etc. they're tempted by Satan to do the opposite, and they succumb. Their eyes are thus turned from God to their own person. They feel naked in front of God and one another.

Self-expression per se is not a bad goal, to be clear. It's simply an incomplete goal in class discussion or any other form of dialog. It will lead to the existential feeling of nakedness because it will insist that we look to ourselves for success rather than to our classmates, teacher, or God. Self-expression will tempt us to do things like strain our interpretation of the text being discussed to appear novel or clever. Or it may keep us so focused on what we might say wrong that we say nothing at all.

So what's the solution? As we know, God provides Adam and Eve a sacrifice to cover their nakedness. More to it, he gives them a promise, a word on which to turn their eyes (Gen 3:15). The entire Old Testament, in fact, is God's call for his people to turn their eyes from themselves (i.e. every man doing right in his own eyes) back to him and his word. This is why Jesus sums up the entire law as (1) loving God with all your heart, mind, strength and (2) loving your neighbor as yourself. God is calling humanity back to a radically extrospective life—focused outside of ourselves on God and neighbor.

Thus, every conversation we have, including those conversations around the Harkness table, should have a higher goal than mere self-expression. By making self-expression subservient to other goods, a student can focus on goals such as truth (centered on God) and love (centered on neighbor).

As a result, we leave discussions not introspectively asking, "How did I do?" Instead, truth will require we evaluate our words using the text being discussed, logic, God, etc. And love will have us ask "were my comments helpful to my peers?" Both metrics (truth and love) will take our eyes off of ourselves.

Of course, simply teaching students to reset their goals in class discussion can't ultimately alleviate their vulnerability; such is the cost of exposing ideas, dreams, and hearts to others. But perhaps by turning our eyes away from ourselves—to our classmates, the text, God—we'll become less aware of our nakedness.

Then, the classroom can be a place of safety and respect, mutual encouragement and generosity. Students won't speak merely to express themselves, but will contribute to aid their peers, find the truth, and understand and enjoy the world. Like Adam and Eve before the Fall, students can have their eyes captivated by the beauty of creation and the majesty of the Creator.

23

LORD OF THE MIDDLE RINGS

"I'm glad you guys moved in by Halloween or it would have been a year before we met!" Those were the first words my neighbor spoke to my wife and me as her daughter held out a basket waiting for a King Size Snickers (first impressions, etc.). She wasn't wrong: the next time we spoke was the following Halloween as her daughter held out her basket waiting for a Fun Size Snickers (don't judge us!).

In our hurried, isolated lives, the opportunities to interact with our neighbors grow fewer and fewer. It turns out, this new normal isn't just problematic for individuals, or even neighborhoods: New research is showing it's actually a threat to the body politic at large. The communal fabric of America seems like it might be unraveling, but the church is uniquely equipped to mend it by being a prophetic witness for the common good.

Let me back up. Alexis de Tocqueville, who would have celebrated his 213th birthday this week, had the keen insight that America's social life is the hallmark of its Democracy. Instead of being a "top-down" Monarchy, the burgeoning

Republic was "bottom-up." The genius of the American experiment, as far as Tocqueville was concerned, was the idea of "townships."

In his book The Vanishing Neighbor, Marc Dunkelman refers to this phenomenon by a different name. Instead of "townships" he refers to "middle rings" of social life. "Inner rings" of social engagement mostly include immediate family—your husband, wife, siblings, kids, parents, etc. "Outer rings," on the other hand, refer to relationships with people you don't live near or who you might not even know—your status as a citizen, membership in a political party, an affinity group or fandom you're part of, your professional network, etc.

Middle rings, however, are usually formal or informal voluntary institutions that help shape your daily life—groups like the Lions Club, churches, carpools, or homeowners associations, for example. The strength of these robust middle rings is part of what caused the cleavage between the Colonials and the Brits, leading to the American revolution. And as far as Tocqueville was concerned, strong, healthy middle rings were what made American politics functional.

Today, much is made out of the collapse of the nuclear family (the inner ring), but Dunkelman points to data that paints a more complicated picture. Indeed, parents are actually spending more time with their kids now than twenty or thirty years ago, not less.

For example, while 50 percent of parents had weekly conversation with their children in 1986, today some 67 percent of mothers report having daily contact with their adult children. Even as many of us spend more time interacting with our inner rings, social media naturally pulls us toward our outer rings, connecting us with, say, fellow sports fans from across the country.

The upshot of the problem is this: If we are spending more time with our immediate families (inner rings) and committing more of our identity or our sense of self to looser, larger affinity groups (outer rings), that's likely to mean we're investing less of our time and energy into our townships, our neighbors, or our "middle rings."

And that's a problem, because those "middle ring" relationships have always been the best way to learn to talk to, understand and even care about people who think very differently— the sort of cooperation that's required for a Republic to work.

G.K. Chesterton's commendation of townships on a human scale is instructive:

"The man who lives in a small community lives in a much larger world. He knows much more of the fierce varieties and uncompromising divergences of men. The reason is obvious. In a large community we can choose our companions. In a small community our companions are chosen for us."

For as tense as family relationships can sometimes be, in the grand scheme of things, our inner ring tends to think and act a lot like we do; and we, of course, largely self-select our outer rings. So if we want to understand the "fierce varieties and uncompromising divergences of men," we can only get that knowledge from those relationships in the middle ring of society. As goes the middle ring—Tocqueville's townships or Richard John Neuhaus' intermediate institutions—so goes politics at large.

The problem is that the one ring that can give us such exposure is currently emaciated, forcing us to exist in louder and louder echo chambers. Says Dunkelman:

"A networked society doesn't bring people with different experiences into contact with one another. Natural rhythms once put Americans from different stations in touch at the store, on the street, in the

newspaper, even at church. Until fairly recently, the cross section of people who lived near one another passed the same billboards, watched the same television shows, and listened to the same radio stations. And so, whatever divided them—issues of race or ethnicity, political creed or religious affiliation—they were more familiar, if only perfunctorily, with the way other people approached the world."

It's here that the church has a unique role to play in the renewal of the Republic. In his book A New Heaven and a New Earth, J. Richard Middleton points out that Revelation 21:3 shifts from the singular to the plural in reference to God's people:

"And I heard a loud voice from the throne saying, 'Behold, the dwelling place of God is with man [singular]. He will dwell with them, and they will be his peoples [plural], and God himself will be with them as their God."'

This shift, says Middleton, shows, "the general thrust of the biblical story, which expands the boundaries of the covenant people to include all humanity." In the Old Testament, we learn that the children of Abraham will be as many as the stars in the sky and the sand on the seashore. (Gen 22:17).

The surprise of the New Testament is that, through the New Covenant, those children will be made up of people from every tribe, tongue and nation. (Rev 5:9) In retrospect, God's all-embracing mission could be seen in the earliest pages of Scripture, as Old Testament scholar Alec Motyer puts it:

"From the very beginning we see that whenever God narrowed his purpose down to the particular, it was in order that he might bring his grace to the universal... The Covenant which began with one man Noah, came to be expressed, after the Flood, in worldwide terms (Gen. 9:12–13) and to be symbolized by the world-embracing rainbow."

Thus the biblical story from Abraham forward can be

summed up as moving from a person (Abraham) to a people (Israel) to a person (Jesus) to all peoples (the multi-ethnic church). Currently, we're living in the "peoples" part of the story, the final and climactic act. This can be seen by looking at where the church is located globally: 26% in Europe, 37% in the Americas, 24% in sub-Saharan Africa, and 13% in Asia and the Pacific. Of course, you can see the same reality by looking at local churches in which multiple families, races and cultures are represented.

While Revelation 21:3 reminds us that the global church is not an inner ring made up of a particular family or blood type, it should also remind local churches that they are not outer rings united by shared political or socio-economic factors. At its best, the local church will reflect at least some of the beauty and diversity of the global church.

Indeed, the church is nothing less than a sign of the present in-breaking of Jesus' inclusive reign. It's a sign that when Christ went down to the grave he secured the treasure once buried in a field. It's a sign that the leaven of the kingdom is working its way through the dough of the world. Indeed, the melting of homogeneous worship can only mean the Spring of Pentecost is here; the King is summoning his peoples. Even if every other middle ring crumbles, local churches can stand firm as places where people of every color and background gather. The saved can't be siloed.

While a local church should by no means be the only middle ring to which a Christian belongs, it is the only one with such a supernatural origin, and thus the only one in which a Christian can fully trust, particularly at a time in which mediating institutions are eroding at such a dizzying speed. After all, it was not the Lions Club that Jesus told us could stand against the gates of hell. Unlike other mediating institutions, "the Church does not live by its organizations and its programs" as Lesslie Newbigin reminds us. Rather, it "lives by the word of God given to it as the word spoken and acted."

It behooves Christians committed to stewarding their civic responsibilities well to rededicate themselves to the local church. I'm preaching to myself here: Why do I feel the need to wait until next Halloween to talk to my neighbor when I'm trained each Sunday to show hospitality to those I don't know? Simply in the act of breaking bread and drinking wine with the proverbial other, the church not only undermines the tribal zeitgeist that seems to have gutted our middle rings, we also mend the tear in the fabric of the Republic—thus fulfilling our calling to be a prophetic witness for the common good.

24

SACRED WORK IN A SECULAR WORLD

S everal weeks ago, a picture of a man working at Trader Joe's went viral. At first glance, it was hard to tell what was worthy of note in the picture—a man simply standing near a cash register. It turns out, the picture went viral not because of what the man was doing, but because of who he was: Geoffrey Owens, who played Elvin Tibideaux in the Cosby Show. Once the picture brought Owens back into the spotlight, he addressed the phenomenon on Good Morning America:

This business of my being this 'Cosby' guy who got shamed for working at Trader Joe's, that's going to pass. ... But I hope what doesn't pass is this idea ... this rethinking about what it means to work, the honor of the working person and the dignity of work...There is no job that's better than another job. It might pay better, it might have better benefits, it might look better on a resume and on paper, but actually it's not better. Every job is worthwhile and valuable, and if we have a kind of a rethinking about that because of what's happened to me, that would be great.

Is Every Job Sacred?

I'm not sure anyone who heard Owens' remarks doubted that they were beautiful; the question is, are they true? Is every job really worthwhile and valuable? Is there something about the nature of working itself that carries with it inherent meaning and dignity? To answer that question, it might be helpful to back up a little and ask, "Where does the idea that all work is sacred come from?" Cambridge professor Owen Chadwick points to the 16thCentury:

> *The Reformation made all secular life into a vocation of God. It was like the baptism of the secular world. It refused any longer to regard the specially religious calling of a priest or monk as higher in moral scale than the calling of a cobbler or of a prince. Christian energy was turned away from the still and the contemplative towards action. The man who would leave the world turned into the man who would change it.*

Anyone familiar with Martin Luther will be sympathetic to his portrait of the Reformation. It was Luther, after all, who claimed that the milkmaid's milking was a service to God just as the preacher's preaching was a service to God. Of course, this only kicks the ball down the road; we're left now asking of the Reformers the same question we were asking of Owens, namely: why is it that every job is sacred? To answer that, we have to back up even further, as far as one can back up, in fact —to the creation of the world.

In Genesis 1:1-2:1 we're given an order to creation: day 1, night and day; day 2, the sky and sea; day 3, land and vegetation; day 4, the sun and the moon; day 5, sea creatures and birds; day 6, animals and humans, and on day 7, God rests. At first glance, this ordering seems strictly historical: Moses lists the creatures in the order in which they were created. On a deeper reading, which by no means necessarily negates the first reading, Moses is giving an order to creation that goes beyond the history of realty and touches on the teleology of reality.

Let me explain: days 1-3 are spheres, days 4-6 are corresponding sovereigns—night and day (day 1) are "governed" by the sun and moon (day 4), the sky and the sea (day 2) are governed by birds and fish (day 5), and land and vegetation (day 3) are governed by animals and, most importantly, mankind (day 6).

It's by examining this passage that we can finally understand the inherent dignity of work. It's here that we see (1) God rules over all and (2) he rules through us.

God Rules Over All

First, God rules over all. In Hebrew, the ending of most words sounds similar, unlike English. Thus, rhyming isn't an optimal vehicle for poetry in the Old Testament. Instead, poetry is conveyed through structure, as in the creation account. The first three days are spheres in need of filling, and the last three days are sovereigns in need of kingdoms. But what about the 7th day? Surely God is more like a sovereign than a sphere, but to what dominion does he correspond?

To ask the question is to answer it: Yahweh has no sphere; about this Moses is clear. Unlike other ancient Near Eastern gods, Yahweh isn't over one part of the world, or one thing in the world—like water or fire—no, Yahweh rules over everything, every sphere is his.

Psalm 103 is the interpretive key to Genesis 1-2, it seems to me. Just take verse 19, "The Lord has established his throne in heaven, and his kingdom rules over all." The 7th day shows us that God is in control; his empire is all-inclusive.

Of course, most Christians aren't tempted to view Yahweh as a tribal God—as if his powers extend only to the ends of a particular region. Yet, Moses' words still prick our hearts if we're sensitive enough to hear his rebuke. We, like the ancient Israelites, are tempted to view God's reign as limited to one particular sphere.

Our God may not be bound by region, but he is bound by religion. We think Scripture is true and Jesus is in charge, etc. But it's a particular kind of truth and a particular kind of authority, religious. It affects us only in our private, devotional lives. His instructions apply to holy things, but common things are beyond his purview.

This is problematic because, in a certain sense, the whole word is a sacred temple—everything is holy. Indeed, the same words used to describe the Lord in the tabernacle (Lev. 26:12; Deut. 23:14-15; 2 Sam. 7:6-7) are used of God's "walking back and forth" in Eden (Gen. 3:8). While this reading may sound novel, the book of Jubilees noted this nearly a hundred years before the birth of Christ: "And [Noah] knew that the garden of Eden was the holy of holies and the dwelling of the LORD."

The witness of the whole of Scripture is this: God isn't limited to a particular place—be it the tabernacle, the temple, or the church building. We never leave his rule because we never leave his reign. Isaiah 66:1-2a is instructive,

> This is what the LORD says: "Heaven is My throne, and earth is My footstool. What kind of house will you build for Me? Or where will be My place of repose? Has not My hand made all these things? And so they came into being, declares the LORD..."

Thus, even if we were able to compartmentalize work and faith, it's no matter because God claims every compartment. Viewing our office complex just as much under the rule of God as our worship service may strike our modern ears as extreme, but Dorothy Sayers points out that the alternative is disastrous:

> [The church] has allowed work and religion to become separate departments, and is astonished to find that, as result, the secular work of the world is turned to purely selfish and destructive ends, and that the greater part of the world's intelligent workers have become irreligious, or at least, uninterested in religion.

God rules over everything—work, play, sex, child rearing, lawyering, doctoring, cleaning, peaching—all of it. The earth is the lord's and the fullness thereof. This is all fine and good, but perhaps we've merely begged the question thus far: how does God rule? That brings us to our second point: God rules through us.

God Rules Through Us

While it's true to say that God has no particular sphere—the whole of creation is his dominion—it's not true to say that God has no sovereigns. Indeed, while it is God that brightens the sky, it is God working through the sun. Each sovereign (created on days 4-6) is a servant of God. The earth is ruled by God, no doubt, but it's ruled by God through man's activity in the world. We're called to activity not passivity. To quote James Skillen:

> The powerful import of acknowledging God's ordinances is precisely that we must work at obeying them; in other

words, we must shape history in accord with those ordinances and not merely ride through history proclaiming that they exist.

Adam's first job will put flesh on this principle. To name something in the Ancient Near East was to take ownership of the thing. This is why God often changes people's names in Scripture. By tasking Adam with the job of naming the animals, God was allowing Adam to partner with him in the rule of creation.

God made creation alone, to be sure, but he doesn't cultivate it alone. No, he uses the insights, creativity, energy, and efforts of mankind. The cultural mandate given to Adam in Genesis 1:28 and Genesis 2:15 and given again to Noah in Genesis 9:1 is a divine invitation to us all—his creatures—to finish in history what God started at creation. Abraham Kuyper put it beautifully:

> Creation was fashioned by God, fashioned with life that surges and scintillates in its bosom, fashioned with the powers that lie dormant in its womb. Yet, lying there, it displayed but half its beauty. Now, however, God crowns it with humanity, who awakens its life, arouses its powers, and with human hands brings to light the glory that once lay locked in its depths but had not yet shone on its countenance.

Said differently, mankind is God's vice-regent. Every sovereign, every ruler, should see his or her authority as derivative of the ultimate ruler, Yahweh. Psalm 2: 10-12 says as much:

> Therefore, you kings, be wise; be warned, you rulers of the

earth. Serve the Lord with fear and celebrate his rule with trembling. Kiss the son, or he will be angry and your way will lead to your destruction, for his wrath can flare up in a moment. Blessed are all who take refuge in him.

We're used to thinking of God working through some people's jobs—we sometimes call ministers vicars for precisely this reason: they're working vicariously on behalf of God. Yet, again, it's not only the religious sphere that's governed by God, it's every sphere. Thus, in a way, we are all vicars; we're all priests in God's service.

We've already noted that Eden was a sort of proto-temple, it follows that Adam—the first worker—was a proto-priest. As a matter of fact, the same Hebrew word used of Adam's working (שמר) in the garden (Gen. 2:15) is used of the priest's work in the tabernacle (Num. 3:7).

I said earlier that Psalm 103 is the interpretive key to the creation account. It's worth noting that after the Psalmist says that God is ruling all (V. 19), he goes on in the following three verses to insist that every creature is thus summoned to do God's will:

Praise the Lord, you his angels, you mighty ones who do his bidding, who obey his word. Praise the Lord, all his heavenly hosts, you his servants who do his will. Praise the Lord, all his works everywhere in his dominion.

God is ruling, but he's ruling through us. Again, the Reformers are helpful here, even as they're often misunderstood. When the likes of Luther and Calvin and Cranmer insisted on the priesthood of all believers, they emphatically were not trying to un-spiritualize the sacred. To the contrary, they were trying to re-spiritualize the secular. Historian David Hopper says this regarding Martin Bucer's view on the matter:

> *Vocation was, for Bucer, the necessary result of a restored order of creation, to wit, a disciplined service and love of neighbor—and all creatures—in this life, once freed, as in Luther, from concern for merit, but one integrated also into ongoing judgments about service to the well-being of the commonwealth.*

The reformers recognized that Adam's cultivation of the garden was just as much a vocation as was Eli's keeping of the temple. With Geoffrey Owens, the Reformers would have insisted:

"There is no job that's better than another job. It might pay better, it might have better benefits, it might look better on a resume and on paper, but actually it's not better. Every job is worthwhile and valuable."

Thus All Work Is Sacred

Finally, we're able to answer the question we asked at the beginning: why is all work sacred? Because (1) God rules over all and (2) he rules through us. We don't have to add meaning to our work, like pepper to a meal. No, we discover meaning inherent in our work. If God's rule is as expansive and if his methods are as mundane as Genesis 1 implies, then we can see how all work can be done as unto the Lord. Dorothy Sayers is again helpful:

> Let the Church remember this: that every maker and worker is called to serve God in his profession or trade – not outside it. The Apostles complained rightly when they said it was not

right they should leave the word of God and serve tables; their vocation was to preach the word. But the person whose vocation it is to prepare the meals beautifully might with equal justice protest: It is not right for us to leave the service of our tables to preach the word.

THINK ABOUT IT, as people came to John the Baptist to hear about the coming Messiah, he didn't say to the tax collectors, "quit your job and go to seminary." No, he said, "Collect no more than is appointed you" (Lk. 3:13). Likewise, when soldiers heard the good news, John didn't have them trade their sword for a scroll. No, he said, "Rob no one by violence or by false accusation, and be content with your wages" (Lk. 3:14).

Finding Your Vocation

In what follows, then, I want to gesture toward what this sacred view of vocation might look like practically. How can we see our jobs as bankers and janitors and lawyers and waiters as callings from God? I'll try to answer that question by giving four pieces of advice: (1) look outside, (2) look inside, (3) look broadly, and (4) look particularly.

First, look outside. Where has God placed you? To whom were you born? What are the conditions of your house, your backyard, your neighborhood? That's where you'll find your vocation. I like how David Brooks puts it:

We don't create our lives; we are summoned by life. The important answers are not found inside, they are found outside. This perspective begins not within the autonomous self, but with the concrete circumstances in which you happen to be embedded. Your job is to figure certain things out: What does this environment need in order to be made whole? What is it that needs repair? What tasks are lying around waiting to be performed?

ARE PEOPLE YOU KNOW COLD? Maybe your vocation is glove making. Are people you know in need of guidance and wisdom? Maybe your vocation is teaching. The point here isn't that you have to meet every need you see, but it is to say that your vocation will be birthed out of the pain you feel when you look at the needs of your neighbors. All work is ministry, all ministry is service.

While it's perhaps easier to see the "service" component in some professions, perhaps those in the non-profit world, all work is in essence service. This is why I don't like it when I hear CEO's of companies talking about "giving back," as if they've robbed us of something, but now through their charitable donations will offer a part of the bounty back to us. If I pay $40 for a haircut, that's because I thought the service the barber could offer me was worth $40. Likewise, the barber felt that the $40 I could offer was worth his time.

Who was robbed in this exchange? No one. I, the customer, was served. Just by bringing his skillset and time to the marketplace the barber gave back to society. If someone is willing to pay for your labor, you're providing a service; you're giving back. This isn't to say there's not a role for charity in corporations. My point is simply that we can't draw a sharp line between charity and business and call one giving and one taking. Regardless of whether or not you work at a 501©3, insofar as the exchange is voluntary, your job is one of service.

Second, look inside. It's not enough to recognize a need; we also must have the desire and skillset to meet the need. I love Frederick Buechner's advice on how to find your calling:

...the kind of work God usually calls you to is the kind of work (a) that you need most to do and (b) that the world most needs to have done. ... The place God calls you to is the place where your deep gladness and the world's deep hunger meet

I'M THANKFUL FOR DOCTORS—THEY diagnose us, they mend us, they care for us—yet, I would never want to be a doctor. Even as a child blood made me squirm. To this day, going to a hospital makes my stomach turn. My sister, on the other hand, was never sick on the days we dissected a pig or a frog in school. Now she's in medicine and I'm not because our subjective feelings about the career differed, not because we disagreed on the objective goodness of the job. That which brings her gladness brings me dread, and visa versa.

Too many people get stuck in a vocational rut because they know they should think the work is worthwhile, yet they just aren't excited by it. Ecclesiastes 2:24 points to the role of joy in work: "A person can do nothing better than to eat and drink and find satisfaction in their own toil. This too, I see, is from the hand of God."

Look inside yourself, what sort of toil gives you satisfaction? Of course, this side of the resurrection, no job will perfectly match our internal calling—there will always be, at best, a slight disunity between our vocation and our work. Still, we can pursue satisfying work, even as we do so realistically.

Third, look broadly. By this I mean that we ought to connect our particular vocation with God's overarching mission in the world. How do all the spheres relate to one another? There are all sorts of studies on the role purpose and contribution play in workers' productivity. If people are told to dig a hole then fill the hole back in, with no reason behind it, they're obviously not going to dig as quickly as a person digging their own well.

It behooves us, then, to understand ourselves as subcontractors. Our work is connected to, but not identical with, God's work in the world. Victor Lee Austin says it well in his beautiful book, *Up With Authority*:

> A real authority will be seen as a person who acts 'with authority,' that is, as a person who is herself 'under' authority. This means that a real authority is not seen as an individual isolated from a larger context. A real authority is not a lone person at the top of a pyramid of power. Rather, she is herself related to other mini-societies and other more encompassing societies. To be an authority is to be connected within the complex web of interrelationships that God has given so that humans may be free. An authority within a given society connects that society's good to the larger human good.

FINALLY, look particularly. When one does the first step of discerning a vocation—when one "looks outside," as it were—it can often feel daunting. There is so much wrong with the world, so much pain, so much disorder, it can lead to one of two negative consequences—exhaustion or apathy. We'll be tempted, perhaps, to do something only Jesus can do: bear the weight of the world's pain on our shoulders.

Obviously untenable, we'll be left at the end of the day weighted down, discouraged, exhausted. Or perhaps we'll be tempted towards apathy. If there's one empty water bottle at the park, we'll bend over and pick it up. If there's a sea of litter, what good will it do to through away one little water bottle? Thus we do nothing. Brian J. Walsh calls us to a better way:

"Build houses in a culture of homelessness. Plant gardens in polluted and contested soil. Get married in a culture of sexual consumerism. Make commitments in a world where we want to always keep our options open. Multiply in a world of debt. Have children at the end of history. Seek shalom in a violent world of geo-political conflict and economic disparity. This is Jeremiah's word to the exiles. This is Jeremiah's subversive word to us. And in this vision we just might see, with Jeremiah, a future with hope."

God doesn't hold us responsible for every beat-up traveler that's ever been left on the side of the road, only the one's by which we pass—he calls him or her our neighbors. Are we stewarding our unique, particular talents well? Are we caring for our home? Are we making our cubicles more beautiful, our meals more delicious, our customers more satisfied, our legal briefs more just, our patients more well, our roads more clean, our crops more productive, our neighborhoods more safe? Fight the battle in which God has placed you and trust the war to him.

In Conclusion

Look outside, where has God placed you? Look inside, what skills and passions has God given you? Look broadly, what is God doing in the world? And look particularly; in what ways can you cause the kingdom to be, even if only a little, more visible in the sphere in which God has made you a sovereign. Because, to quote Wendell Berry, "There is no 'better place' than this, not in this world. And it is by the place we've got, and our love for it, and our keeping of it, that this world is joined to Heaven."

Work—even work at Trader Joe's—is sacred because God rules over all, and he rules through us.

25

FOLLOWING ROB BELL: THE EDGES OF FAITH AND THE CENTER OF THE ZEITGEIST

Several days ago, Kent Dobson, successor at Rob Bell's famous Mars Hill Bible Church, stepped down as teaching pastor. He opened his announcement/sermon by reading the Scriptural story which gives name to the church, the account at Mars Hill. Dobson says when he first came to Mars Hill, he was animated by Paul's example of cultural engagement. Paul quoted the poets of the people; he spoke their language. Dobson said he understood Paul to be preaching a traditional gospel message but using different, more relevant, packaging.

Likewise, he said the church was meant to have the same gospel but deliver the message in a more hip way. Specifically, he wanted a "cool church" with "cooler shoes" than the traditional church down the road. However, Dobson said he not only began to question the packaging of traditional "church," but also the message – the gospel. To fully understand his evolution he says, "you'll have to read my memoirs." The Cliffs-Notes version, for those of us who can't wait, goes thusly:

I have always been and I'm still drawn to the very edges of religion and faith and God. I've said a few times that I don't even know if we know what we mean by God anymore. That's the edges of faith. That's the thing that pulls me. I'm not really drawn to the center. I'm not drawn to the orthodox or the mainstream or the status quo... I'm always wandering out to the edge and beyond.

If you don't have time to watch the whole sermon, just picture Portlandia doing a Dane Cook spoof. Slouched in his flannel shirt, he swivels on his chair as he muses about his restlessness, his angst, and his exploration into the unknown.

I don't know how he actually came off in the room, in the moment. But watching from a distance, he seemed like a romantic vagabond, a sensitive soul longing for a home he's never known—perhaps like Huckleberry Finn if Huck were super into Spiced Chai Lattes and self-indulgent journaling.

Of course, I'm not opposed to someone discerning a vocational shift. Not everyone who leaves the pastorate does so out of cowardice or sin. What I am opposed to is the supposition behind his departure—the reason he gives for leaving. For Dobson, he's been on a journey which started one place and is leading him to another; specifically, to the edges of faith. In actual fact, he's exactly where he's always been.

His self-professed goal was always to be the cool pastor with the cool shoes. It's not that he's journeyed away from the "center" of faith. No, he's just stayed in the center of the zeitgeist—in the "mainstream" of a culture which is rapidly leaving Christian orthodoxy behind. He's not energized with a boyish, effrontery audacity, he's paralyzed with fear.

To his church, he paints himself like a modern-day Ferdinand Magellan, ready to explorer the great spiritual unknown.

Motivated by nothing but curiosity and bravery, he's boldly setting his sails toward the choppy waters which stand between what is and what could be. This is the point at which I take issue.

When was the last time Pastor Dobson talked with someone on a college campus, in a gym, or in a coffee shop? Does he really think the "open" and "inclusive" vision he's casting is novel? Is the "status quo" really Christian orthodoxy among Dobson's peers? As a young, fit, white, upper-middle class male, Dobson's sermon is not a rebellion to his culture. It's a product of his culture.

The mystery and romance he attempts to conjure around his spiritual evolution is laughable to anyone with a television. He's not moving forward into the unknown; he's sitting perfectly still in the safe, cozy space where Oprah is queen, tolerance is the law, and anyone with a firm opinion on just about anything is suspect.

Perhaps this whole episode wouldn't be as disconcerting if there weren't pastors in other parts of the world who actually are venturing into the unsure world of faithfulness to Christ, at the risk of their very lives. It's difficult to hear a shepherd spin his actions as brave or noble when he's hiking up his tunic and making for the hills, leaving his sheep for hungry wolves.

While our brothers and sisters in the majority world continue to meet in caves and barns in the face of imminent danger, many of those called to the shepherding office in the developed world lack the gall to hide the sheep and stand before the wolves with staff in hand. They can't stomach the sound of fur parting with flesh—the whimpering is too much. They would rather let the sheep be eaten than seem like boring, dorky-sneaker-wearing shepherds. The prophetic voice of the American church has gone hoarse.

In a world where pastors wait with bended knees and clenched eyes for their heads to roll down the sandy slopes of a Libyan beach, the complacent, comfortable, Western church must reset her vision of bravery as it relates to the pastorate. There was a time—even in the West—where cultural capital was gained by being a Christian. In those days, there were indeed men who risked everything to leave orthodoxy—one thinks of the great George MacDonald. However, those days are long gone, and Dobson is no MacDonald. If he wants to be known as an adventurer, Dobson is a couple decades late to the "I'm just not into religion" voyage. That land has been claimed and settled. Dobson's predecessor is already giving surfing lessons to the tourists who want to visit.

These days, the real adventurers are those who set sail for the risky land of Christian orthodoxy. The real brave men and women are those who consistently go to church, observe the sacraments, hear the word, and submit themselves to the discipline of the church. In an age of autonomy, it's those who subject their thoughts, behaviors, and passions to an exclusive Sovereign that are the brave few. Those may not be the memoirs we're interested in today, but they'll be the ones that last tomorrow.

26

STOP GOING TO HEAVEN

Recently, the boy who came back from heaven admitted in a letter that he made the whole thing up. Setting aside the prescience of the boy's name (Malarkey), and the fact that this whole debacle is remarkably similar to the *Boy Meets World* episode in which Cory has to come clean about the fire he supposedly helped put out, there are actually some valuable lessons to be learned. Indeed, the boy's letter is full of courage, humility, and good-sense.

At the end of the day, the issue has never been about whether one particular boy was lying or being truthful. Actually, the problematic issue isn't even whether it's possible to go to heaven and come back. The problem is with the culture which glorifies such heaven-encounters; a culture which places a higher premium on human experience than divine promises. The problem is a product of a church which has so conflated one's "testimony" with the "gospel presentation," that the wilder the story of "coming into the Kingdom of Heaven," the more assurance one can have.

Ultimately, this subjective-experientialism is not a publishing problem; it's a worship problem. We go to church and see baptisms which claim to have little to do with God's covenantal promises to the one being baptized, and everything to do with man's promises to God. The sacraments have become the rainbow we offer to God, promising to never flood Him with our betrayal. What's more, we've traded songs about God's immovable, great, mighty character for songs about our great, immovable, mighty affection for Him.

Of course, it's appropriate to sing songs about our love for God; and the sacraments are certainly "communal," thus have an anthropological dimension. The problem, as B.B. Warfield might say, is that we've become a people who think of ourselves as saved by faith alone, rather than saved by faith in Christ alone. Our hope has shifted from the object of our faith to the subjective experience of the object. Is it any wonder our children think they have to drum up a "heaven" experience to have any assurance of faith?

Naturally, there are many ways in which to answer the question, "how did evangelical worship get to such an anemic state in the first place?" One historian, Daryl Hart, shows the line going back to the mid-20th century:

"THE LEADERS of the neo-evangelical movement of the 1940's hoped to give new significance to the word and in so doing did not spend much time thinking about one aspect of the Christian life—namely, worship—that has remarkable power to unite believers across generations and cultures on a weekly basis. They relied instead on the repertoire of worship practices inherited from American revivalism,

which depended heavily on music to rouse seekers to walk the aisle and believers to ratchet up their devotion."

IN OTHER WORDS, THROUGH "ROUSING" and "ratcheting," through experience, our worship became an attempt to emotionally go up to God in heaven, not experience Him coming down in word and sacrament. Certainly, adaptations of 19th century revivalistic methods in the 20th century are a good place to start. However, as far back as the 17th century Matthew Henry was dealing with a church-culture trying to go up to heaven. Says Henry in his March 6, 1692 sermon:

"BELIEVE the revelation of the Word concerning the riches of Christ and his readiness to give it out to us. Say not, 'How shall I go to Christ into heaven?' No, the Word is nigh you (Rom. 10:8). 'Tis Christ in the promise that you are to be close with. Come to him as Joseph's brethren, to him for corn, humbled, submissive. Receive Christ and his fullness, give up yourselves to him."

OF COURSE, the problem is even older than the 17th century. The problem goes back to the people Moses found when he came down from Mount Sinai. Unsure as to when he was coming down with God's word, they built an idol to worship in the meantime. It goes back to Babel, when the people attempted to build a mechanism tall enough to reach heaven's door. Indeed, ever since being banished from Eden, man has attempted various self-rescue projects. Man is more comforted by his own efforts upward than God's action downward.

So, what's the solution to our "going to heaven" problem?

Well, in the same sermon Henry offers the means of grace as a crucial component to the solution. He calls the "ordinances" the "golden pipes by which the oil of grace is conveyed." The evangelical church must recover a liturgy which respects the ways in which God has chosen to commune with His people.

You see, we don't need a vision of heaven, or even an incredible experience at a retreat, to have assurance. We can have assurance because God has come down to us. In His Son, God climbed down Jacob's ladder. Contra Plato, the solution to the human predicament was not physical flesh becoming an ethereal "word."

No, the Word became flesh. We don't go to heaven, heaven comes to us. To go to heaven, to be anointed with the oil of grace, one must stop trying to find golden pipes other than the ones God has provided. Until such reforms are made in our worship, we can only expect more Boy Meets World reruns.

27

INVITING UNCLE SAM INTO THE SANCTUARY

On an appointed day Herod put on his royal robes, took his seat upon the throne, and delivered an oration to them. And the people were shouting, 'The voice of a god, and not of a man!' Immediately an angel of the Lord struck him down, because he did not give God the glory, and he was eaten by worms and breathed his last.-Acts 12: 21-23

First Baptist Church Dallas recently hosted a "Celebrate Freedom Concert" featuring their pastor, Robert Jeffress, and President Trump, who Jeffress recently called "one of the great patriots of our modern era." Last Sunday, FBC celebrated "Freedom Sunday;" complete with a presentation of colors, soldiers, guns, patriotic hymns, indoor fireworks, the whole shebang.

While most churches this 4th of July weekend won't try to bust a bottle rocket from the balcony, many will sing the national anthem, pledge their allegiance to the American flag, and maybe even hear a sermon on 1 Peter 2:9 called "A Royal Nation: Brexit 1776." Meanwhile, many other church-goers, myself included, will be mortified by such actions.

To be clear, I'm not opposed to mixing religion and government/politics. For one, it's impossible not to mix the two, just like it's impossible not to mix religion and music or religion and parenting. Religion, as David Dark has so helpfully pointed out, is ever consuming and all present. It's the way we live and move and have our being in the world. It can be seen as easily in our credit card statements as in our church attendance.

Not just Christians, everyone brings religion into government, arguing for or against particular policies based on their own core commitments and values—values not shared by the whole of society, mind you. Asking someone to keep religion out of politics is like asking someone to fly by lifting the chair in which they're sitting off the ground. It sounds swell, but it's impossible.

Even if it were possible to silo religion in the church, away from the public square, Scripture forbids Christians from taking such an approach. The myth of neutrality is promulgated by secularism, not Scripture. That being the case, if the church isn't trying to transform the culture, the culture is succeeding in transforming the church.

You see, the Bible isn't just God's word to the church, it's God's word to the whole world—everyone, everything. So, applying the Bible to every sphere of life (politics, art, family, etc.) isn't involving the church in those areas, it's involving Jesus. And it turns out, Jesus doesn't just claim to be the King of the church, He's King of the cosmos—which includes every square, even public ones. Nicholas Wolterstorff says it well:

. . .

"SINCE THE CONTENT *of Christian theology goes far beyond church and devotional life to life as a whole, and since its addressees extend far beyond church members to humanity in general, its arena must be civil society.*"

I DON'T TAKE ISSUE, then, with the church involving herself in national life. To the contrary, I'm quite happy for the church to take her message into the most sacred of State spaces—pray in Congress, display the 10 Commandments at the courthouse. What I oppose is the State taking her message into the most sacred of church spaces. I oppose that which causes a worship service to be marked more by a folksy, sentimental religiosity than a solemn, joyful reverence.

Bringing religion into government is responsible for William Wilberforce's effort to abolish the slave trade in England and Martin Luther King Jr.'s tireless effort to see all God's children treated equally irrespective of race in America. Bringing government into the church, on the other hand, brought us the ecclesial malaise and kowtowing which allowed Nazis to exterminate Jews on Saturday and receive the Eucharist on Sunday.

Christians are called to persuade the nation with the message of the church, not persuade the church with the message of the nation. One can faithfully use the State to advance the Kingdom, but God help the man who uses the Kingdom to advance the State.

Setting fireworks off in a sanctuary is dangerous, but not just for the obvious reasons. Sure, it may cause someone to lose an eye, but it may also cause someone to lose sight of the purpose of worship, which is far more serious and far more likely.

So, this Sunday let's observe the sacraments, hear the word preached, confess our sins, and sing about the grace and power and goodness of the Lord of all nations. Instead of *This Land is Your Land*, let's sing *This is My Father's World*. Instead of *The Battle Hymn of the Republic*, let's sing *A Mighty Fortress is our God*.

In other words, let's pledge our allegiance solely to Jesus, finding our identity chiefly as heirs of God's Kingdom. In addition to being what we're commanded to do, it also produces what our nation actually needs: citizens attuned to the true, good, and beautiful; shaped by love in worship, sent out to seek the welfare of the city by promoting the common good.

28

CHOOSING A DENOMINATION FOR THE WRONG REASONS

I recently had coffee with a friend who is seriously considering leaving one denomination for another. His reasons for seeking my advice had less to do with my wisdom and more to do with my experience. After growing up in a godly, Baptist home— and then after years of ministry in a healthy Presbyterian Church—I became an Anglican. To be sure, I left the PCA in a good mood, just as I left the SBC before that.

I wouldn't trade my Baptist upbringing for the world, and I still reference the Westminster Confession of Faith almost daily. My transition from the PCA to the Anglican Communion felt more like a skip than a leap. Said differently, my "conversion" wasn't motivated by any perceived weakness in the Presbyterian tradition. I left because of what I saw as the strengths of the Anglican tradition. This, I now believe, was a mistake.

Now, before you go questioning my Anglican bona fides, let me explain. I'm a happy Anglican. I still hold to all of the liturgical and theological positions and interpretations which motivated my realignment in the first place. What I believe was a mistake, looking back, was my optimism. I viewed the baptismal font as half-full, in other words. If I had it to do over again, I would have joined the Anglican Communion for her weaknesses, not her strengths.

If you only choose a denomination because of her "best practices," you'll always be disappointed. Calvin won't be your Presbyter, Cranmer won't be your Bishop, your church will likely not be on Wesley's circuit. Joining a denomination because of her strengths has a way of making the convert somewhat grumpy.

We view ourselves as second generation Israelites in exile, longing for a home we've never known. Depending on what you consider the "promised land," the denomination is too rigid or too lax, too ingrown or too compromising, too modern or too post-modern, too traditional or too progressive. With this mindset, the pastor-brother who does things differently is viewed as a competitor at best, and mere rust on a ship at worst. Churches, further, are simply battle grounds to be won or obstacles to be overcome.

This "competitor" and "battle" mentality is the natural result of choosing a denomination based on "best practices." After all, think of the theological cage fights which brought you to the denomination in the first place. The choice between Catholic and Protestant consisted of a 4th century theologian against a 16th century theologian.

If the Protestant won, you then pitted representatives from various traditions against one another: Calvin v. Arminius, or Whitfield v. Wesley. All of this tussling and you still hadn't landed on a denomination! Now you had to have Schaeffer v. Van Til, or Keller v. Hart, maybe. Each battle got more and more precise, moving from boxing matches, to basketball games, to chess tournaments.

Of course, the problem isn't with the competitions themselves. If there is such a thing as "truth" it's worth finding, and we shouldn't expect to come to it without a busted lip or two. The problem is with the stakes of the fights: namely, denominational loyalty. If Keller beats Hart, you join the PCA instead of the OPC. However, there are people who sound more like Hart than Keller at General Assembly.

Surely, this won't do—after all, Keller won! Your job, then, is to reenact the "Keller v. Hart" match on the floor of GA and in the halls of your church. Again, in the mind of the arguer, the stakes are the same: denominational loyalty. The winner is "in" and the loser is "out."

The alternative to choosing a denomination because of her "best practices" is choosing a denomination because of her "worst practices." Then, your choice isn't between "X 4th century theologian and Y 16th century theologian." You can keep them both!

Rather, you'll decide between "X sin (praying to an icon, say) and Y sin (anemic view of the sacraments, say)." Choose the denomination because, at its worst, it still doesn't command you to do something God forbids or forbid you from doing something God commands. Meticulously account for the "worst" in each denomination, all along the way asking: "can I live with this?"

If you can't live with X in a denomination, then spare everyone the heartache and don't join the denomination which consists of many who hold to X. However, if you're able to live with the state of the denomination, even after evaluating what you perceive to be her "worst practices," then by all means, join! This doesn't mean you can't debate serious theological issues with your brothers and sisters. It simply means that your brothers and sisters are just that, and neither the "winning" nor "losing" party will be excluded from the next family picture.

My friend asked me to get coffee because he wanted advice. After much listening, I simply told him the following: view the baptismal font as half-empty. Sure, love the "best" that your tradition has to offer, but make sure your love is for the denomination you're joining, not the one in your mind. After all, the utopian-denomination of your mind likely never existed in the first place! Don't be so homesick for Eden that you fail to march on to the New Jerusalem. Make your peace with the church's purity, and then do your best to preserve her purity and peace.

29

CAN ST. NICK SAVE CHRISTMAS?

I n the first half of the fourth century, St. Nicholas of Myra punched the Trinity-denying Arius in the face. At least, that's what the memes on my newsfeed say. Regardless of the historicity, the motivation behind its retelling is clear: the true meaning of Christmas has been watered down because a secular, make-believe figure has been elevated to the same level as Jesus. The King of Kings now shares the spotlight with Kris Kringle.

St. Nick Solution

St. Nicholas appears to offer some help. On the one hand, he offers a certain "Christian" flavor to the Santa myth. In the war on Christmas, Christians have a secret weapon. We have a man behind enemy lines, hiding in plain, red-coated sight. Likewise, St. Nick grounds Santa in history. The complaint of Christian parents vis-à-vis Santa has long been: how can we say Jesus and

Santa are real without expecting our kids to doubt the former once they stop believing in the latter?

You can see the appeal of the St. Nick option. Historically, Jesus and St. Nick are both "real" in the same way King Edward IV and Teddy Roosevelt both occupied time and space. Spiritually, Jesus and St. Nick are both "faithful" in the same way Thomas Aquinas and John Bunyan were both Christian.

Once Santa is established as historical, so goes the logic, we needn't worry about our kids believing in Christ today but becoming scorned atheists tomorrow. Similarly, if Santa is a thorough, trinitarian Christian, we needn't worry about hanging our sleigh ornament on a branch under the Bethlehem Star. Both point to Immanuel in their own way. I just don't think this reindeer will fly.

Exalting God Over Santa

Sure, I'm sympathetic to the St. Nick option, and I certainly want to give a brother in Christ his due for going fisticuffs with a heretic. But Santa can't be helped, I believe, because the problem isn't with our faulty view of him. That's not why he overshadows Jesus. Santa overshadows Jesus because we have a faulty view of God.

Even a cursory scan of evangelicalism reveals that many view angels as little more than elves and God as a cosmic Santa Claus: seasonal, jolly, and meritocratic. The St. Nick option assumes Jesus will take his rightful place at Christmas once Santa is brought down to the level of a historical saint. But the real solution isn't lowering Santa to his rightful place; it's exalting God to his. In order to have "more Christ in Christmas" we need less sentimentality in theology—that is, we must see God as the sovereign, holy, and merciful God he is.

Sovereign Over Seasons

Besides an aisle in Hobby Lobby, we restrict Santa's influence to a specific time and place. We tend to do the same thing with God. The Scriptures tell a different story, though: it's incumbent on the rulers of the earth (whether they rule a nation, a business, a family, or an apartment) to serve the Lord in all they do—to "kiss the Son" in allegiance (Ps. 2:12).

The first step in putting Christ back into Christmas is realizing God, unlike Santa, has "creator rights" over everything. He will not be relegated to a "season." The sun never sets on his kingdom, and his reign has no end. Heaven is not the great North Pole in the sky, a distant land to which we occasionally send gift requests; heaven is where God reigns. And one day his reign will so thoroughly invade earth that there will be no need for the sun, for the Son will be its light (Rev. 21:23).

We don't simply go to heaven with our requests; heaven comes to us with an invitation to embrace Christ and a commission to proclaim him.

Holly Over Holly and Jolly

Santa isn't stern or abrasive; he's rosy, fluffy, and jolly. Of course, this is no accident. A committee of the New-York Historical Society designed his image to be warm, approachable, and inviting. This is how we often talk about God. From what he does, to what he loves, to how he responds to sin—our thoughts about God are often based more on what we'd like to be true than on what actually is.

Despite our most earnest wishes, God will not be remade in our image. He is holy and wholly different from his creation. He wasn't committee-designed; he is eternally existent in three persons. If you're waiting to approach his throne until he changes his disposition to suit your sensibilities, you're waiting in vain. God doesn't exist to make us comfortable, and his gospel isn't a marketing pitch—it's a divine summons to repentant faith.

Mercy Over Merit

The logic of Santa is clear. If you've been a good boy or girl, you get a treat; if you've been naughty, you get coal. You get what you deserve. How often do we use God in the same way, as a mere deterrent to doing wrong?

But God's justice system is entirely different than Santa's. Through his death and resurrection, Jesus unites his church to himself, making every reward that's rightfully his available to his bride. Divine mercy isn't simply the turning of a blind eye to naughtiness.

No, Christ shares his Father's lavish gifts by absorbing our punishment in our place. God sent his Son into the mineshaft only to collapse it. Jesus took all the coal there was to give. God only has presents for his children now.

Only Real Solution

Santa Tebowing at a manger in the front yard isn't the solution. We must recognize that the real problem is a folksy religiosity that pulls God the Father down to level of Father Christmas. Until we're able to banish such sappy thinking from our theology and see our Maker as sovereign, holy, and merciful, St. Nicholas is nothing more than a band-aid. In fact, our baptism of Santa may only serve to codify and sanction the real problem.

The "war on Christmas" isn't being waged by those who've forgotten Santa's true identity; it's being waged by those who've forgotten God's.

30

IS SOCIAL JUSTICE JUST?

I f you follow the evangelical blogosphere, you're no doubt aware of the most recent dust-up over the Social Justice Statement. In what follows, I want to briefly explain (1) why I didn't sign the statement and (2) defend the use of the phrase "social justice."

Why I didn't sign the statement

If you actually read the document, it's much more reserved than you might expect. This is also its weakness, however. Words go undefined and assumed, leaving the reader unsure as to who or what is actually being rebuked. And then there's the generally condescending attitude toward any sort of activism:

> And we emphatically deny that lectures on social issues (or activism aimed at reshaping the wider culture) are as vital to the life and health of the church as the preaching of the

gospel and the exposition of Scripture. Historically, such things tend to become distractions that inevitably lead to departures from the gospel.

THE STATEMENT IS full of false dichotomies such as this. Because of the inherent nature of Scripture, the preacher doesn't have to apply the text, per se; rather, he has to show the text's applicability. Thus, the line between expositing the passage and exhorting the people is always blurred.

Indeed, the book of James demolishes the sort of hermeneutic that siloes hearing from doing. I didn't sign the document because I can't tell women working at crisis pregnancy centers across the country that they're distracted. I can't tell them that they're on a slippery slope to gospel-departure. I can't tell them that they should believe what Psalm 139:13 says about babies, but not act upon it.

Of course, God holds us responsible in regards to the faithfulness which we show to our work, not our fruit, but is the preacher really being faithful to his calling if he isn't hoping and praying that the Spirit, through the word, will reshape individuals, families, neighborhoods, indeed "wider cultures?" With Nicholas Wolterstorff, I want to insist,

The church is not merely to wait with grim patience for the new age when the Spirit will fully renew all existence. It must already, here and now, manifest signs of that renewing Spirit.

In Defense of Social Justice

Having said that, however, my goal isn't to attack those critical of social justice. With those critics, I think that the identity politics being practiced on the left and right is an acid that's leaving the fabric of our culture threadbare.

The longer we soak in it, the more the societal trust that's required for a community to flourish disintegrates. Indeed, anyone who's read Karl Marx knows his name isn't being invoked in vain by those critical of our increasingly tribalistic politics.

So while I couldn't in good conscience sign the statement, I don't think those who did are bigoted or uninformed. As I said, my goal isn't to attack the document or its signers. Rather, my goal is to defend the origin and use of the phrase social justice.

As I understand the criticism, "social justice" language is problematic because (1) it has Marxist origins thus imports, at best, problematic categories, and (2) it assumes that's there are multiple kinds of justice, whereas Scripture only speaks of one sort—God's.

The first point will take the least amount of space to refute. As a point of historical fact, one of the first philosophers to use the expression was the Catholic priest Antonio Rosmini, writing in Italy in the 19th century. At places, Rosmini sounds as if he could be responding directly to the recent critics of the phrase:

Justice is not manufactured by human beings, nor can human hands dismantle it. It is prior to laws made by human beings; such laws can only be expressions of justice. Justice is the essence of all laws to such an extent that Saint Augustine had no hesitation in refusing to name as 'law' anything that lacked justice. Nor does authority exist except as a servant of justice.

THE ACTON INSTITUTE is to be commended in their efforts to bring Rosmini's writings back into relevance. While no doubt others use the phrase in a way incongruent with the originator's intent, I seek to defend the sort of social justice about which Rosmini speaks and the Acton Institute, for example, embodies.

The second point will take a bit longer than the first. In an effort to be fair to those critical of the phrase, I'll engage with one of the chief critics directly, Voddie Baucham. Dr. Baucham sums up his point powerfully:

> There's no such thing as 'social justice.' In fact, in the Bible, justice never has an adjective. There's justice and there's injustice, but there's not different kinds of justice.

PERHAPS A STORY WILL BE of help here. I have a good friend who recently made a compelling case for Socialism using Scripture. Toward the end of our conversation, she asked how I could read the book of Acts—in which we see believers having all things in common—and not embrace a forced redistribution of wealth.

Moments earlier, I had said that I believed the government was too far-reaching as it is, so it took her off guard when I conceded that wealth should indeed be redistributed. To not redistribute wealth, I said, would be a tremendous injustice.

"Finally, you #FeelTheBern!" she shouted with joy! Not quite. You see, if a mother and father don't redistribute their income to their children, they're derelict. If they don't freely feed, cloth, and house their toddler, they're unjust. Scripture commands as much, to not obey would be sin. Likewise, giving to your church, as we see in more places than just Acts, is a divine directive.

God doesn't suggest we redistribute our income, he insists. Yet in these instances, it's the family and the church that are the instruments of redistribution. So, to say something is demanded of a person isn't the same thing as saying it's the State's prerogative to enforce said demand.

But more to the point, surely there's a difference between how we share our money with our immediate family and how we share our money with our church community. Our kids will likely require much more than a tenth of our income, after all!

Now, if you're familiar with the Neo-Calvinistic tradition out of which I come, you've already anticipated the two points I was trying to make with my friend: (1) the State isn't the only vehicle for the distribution of justice and (2) we ought not ham-fistedly apply directives given to one institution to another.

There are myriad different spheres of life—schools, cities, clubs, churches, families—each with their own system of governance, their own sovereign, their own code. Indeed, I don't think it would be an equivocation to say each sphere has its own *justice,* if by that we mean that a just way to behave in one sphere might be unjust in another.

For example, we should have compassion on anyone living in poverty, but our responsibility for the impoverished person correlates to how closely the person is related to us, a point Paul makes in 1 Tim 5:8:

If anyone doesn't take care of his own relatives, especially his immediate family, he has denied the Christian faith and is worse than an unbeliever.

A MAN MIGHT BE JUSTIFIED in passing a homeless man on the street without stopping, but if the same man were to pass by his mother begging on the street without stopping, he'd no doubt be unjust in doing so. One action can be just in one context or sphere but unjust in another. The sphere, not only the action, matters.

A pastor ought not imprison a criminal in his vestry—that's the role of the State. A mayor ought not baptize the police chief —that's the role of the church. Likewise, while the description of believers living a life of shared resources in Acts is no doubt prescriptive today, it must be prescribed within the appropriate sphere, namely the church.

None of this is to say that Scripture has nothing to say regarding the State. To the contrary, kings and all civil rulers are beckoned therein to rule justly and govern under the ultimate Lordship of Christ. The Bible speaks to *every* sphere of life, as Abraham Kuyper taught so many of us. A well-ordered society is one in which each sphere is in tune with God's revelation, both special (i.e. Scripture) and general (i.e. Natural Law).

A just society requires more than just one sphere functioning appropriately, it requires all of them working in harmony with one another and the divine order of reality. One can be born into a healthy family that worships in an unhealthy church, just as one can go to a healthy school in an unhealthy city.

Speaking of social justice, then, allows us to speak about the society on a macro level—evaluating more than just the State or the church or the family or the prison system or the school—but analyzing the economy of institutions as a whole, with God's special and general revelation as the grid.

In conclusion, I understand that I'm not likely to convince my friends who are critical of social justice to adopt the phrase. But my hope is more modest than that. My hope is that in showing that the (1) origin and (2) usage of social justice aren't as nefarious as is often claimed, the critics can at least allow for the possibility that not everyone is using the word to smuggle in a Marxist agenda.

31

THESE AREN'T ANIMALS

E arlier this week Donald Trump called a group of immigrants animals—"You wouldn't believe how bad these people are. These aren't people. These are animals." The comment was broadcast far and wide with universal condemnation. A tweet from *The New York Times* was typical,

> Trump lashed out at undocumented immigrants during a White House meeting, calling those trying to breach the country's borders "animals."

THE STATEMENT, it turns out, came on the heels of a comment by Fresno County Sheriff Margaret Mims who was talking about the notorious gang MS-13. In context, it's clear that the

President wasn't speaking of immigrants generally, but of one of the most brutal, vicious gangs in North America particularly.

Perhaps it's still morally questionable to refer to even the most hardened of criminals in such a way, but it's at least not a given. Indeed, it was one of President Obama's great weaknesses that his moral imagination couldn't—or wouldn't—account for violent actors in such stark terms, preferring instead to qualify ostensibly evil acts with the language of mental illness, situational contextualization, etc.

To be sure, if President Obama erred in being too soft in his rhetoric, Trump has no doubt erred in being too hard. The truth is, one could imagine President Trump saying what he did about M-13 about undocumented immigrants carte blanche. He didn't, thankfully, but it's not beyond the realm of possibility, which is why so many were quick to believe it happened.

Of course, defenders of the President weren't surprised by the day's coverage—just another instance of the lamestream media spouting fake news in an effort to undermine the 2016 election. Yet, despite what Sean Hannity may insist, the problem is not, in fact, a unified, faceless conglomerate—"the media"—seeking to take down the President.

Were that the case—were there really two actors, the POTUS and the media, competing against one another in a battle for the public's trust—then the faux reporting wouldn't have happened. There's no doubt that this week was a net loss for the proverbial media. There is even less confidence in journalism this week than there was last week. John Wilson, former editor of *Books and Culture*, was right when he tweeted about the incident,

What makes it even worse is that it is CALCULATED

(calculated in part to provoke critics to say he's contemplating genocide, etc., which hyperbole then generates more support from his base).

So WHILE THE coverage turned out to be a win for the President, it was nevertheless a net gain for those individual journalists and bloggers who got the clicks and eyeballs they were aiming for in the first place. And that's the rub: the problem is less nefarious and more dangerous than the current narrative grants. So long as we exclusively look for those news sources that confirm what we already believe, there will be willing and able writers to whet our appetites with half-true stories (and as our grandmothers taught us, half-truths are just whole-lies in disguise).

Take an example less infused with political heat. Shortly after the infamous Southwest Airlines Flight 1380 required an emergency landing, the front page of various news sources was striking. The top story at CNN read, "Hero pilot is a woman–of course." Compare that with the headline at FOX, "Hero in a Cowboy hat." Both stories were true, but both appealed to the sensibilities of their readership. In other words, the desire wasn't to inform but to draw in readers by reaffirming biases.

This is a good example of the real problem with modern journalism, and "fake news" isn't a helpful description—that shifts the blame to *them* when it belongs to *us*. We're eager to see heroes that share our sensibilities, and news agencies deliver. This can seem fairly benign, like in this case. But the converse is also true: we're hungry to see the other villainized and demeaned, and news agencies deliver on that too, which really is corrosive to our social fabric.

You may not think Donald Trump is morally fit to be President. That's a perfectly acceptable position to hold; it's one I happen to hold myself, in fact. We err when we only look at news which caters to that narrative, refusing to accept troublesome data or twisting the data to fit the conclusions we already hold, which is what happened with the "animals" story. There will always be a supply for that which we demand.

It's true, journalists indeed need more integrity, but so too do we need more empathy. Until we're able to see the villain in our tribe (and, indeed, ourselves) and the hero in the other tribe, we'll keep getting half the story.

32

TALKING THE WEST OFF THE LEDGE

Thus did Western Man decide to abolish himself, creating his own boredom out of his own affluence, his own vulnerability out of his own strength, his own impotence out of his own erotomania, himself blowing the trumpet that brought the walls of his own city tumbling down. -Malcolm Muggeridge

IF YOU COULD BE dictator of America for one day, what would be the first thing you'd do to fix the country? In a recent interview, George Will gave a surprising response to this question, which I'll paraphrase:

I'd make every college student change their major to History and their minor to Contingency Studies.

His point: America did not have to turn out the way it did. The Republic we inhabit is the result of bravery and revolutionary ideas, to be sure, but it's also the result of an often under-appreciated element; namely, *chance*. In his new book, *Suicide of the West: How the Rebirth of Tribalism, Populism, Nationalism, and Identity Politics is Destroying American Democracy*, Jonah Goldberg takes this observation a step further. Not only is the freedom we enjoy a historical anomaly, it's unnatural:

> Capitalism is unnatural. Democracy is unnatural. Human rights are unnatural. God didn't give us these things, or anything else. We stumbled into modernity accidentally, not by any divine plan.

If those of us who believe in providence dismiss his argument out of hand, we do so at our own peril. As Goldberg chronicles, for most of mankind's history, we've lived a tribal, violent existence. That we now view the proverbial "other" with as little skepticism as we do is a feat of monumental proportion. A feat accomplished by what, you ask? Goldberg answers: money. Money made it possible for a person of one tribe to have an exchange with a person of another tribe that was mutually beneficial. The "other" in a free market isn't just a competitor, he's a customer.

Because the peace we have with one another now is incomplete and imperfect, it's easy to view the current state of affairs with contempt. In the age of Trump, with identity politics being practiced by the Left and the Right, Goldberg sees the natural human propensity toward tribalism "coming back with a pitchfork."

We're renovating the Republic with the sledgehammer of populism, knocking down institutions and norms at will, unmindful of which artifacts are structural and which are superficial, which are negotiable and which are load-bearing. Thus, the structural-integrity of the West has been compromised, perhaps irreparably, by those seeking to improve it. No, the current system isn't perfect, but it's better than an infinite number of alternatives that seemed inevitable a relatively short time ago.

There's a famous story in which Benjamin Franklin is asked what sort of government the delegates at the Constitutional Convention are attempting to create, to which he responds, "A republic, if you can keep it." Goldberg's proposal for keeping the Republic lies not in specific policy proposals—he offers relatively few in the book—but in a disposition: gratitude.

Illustratively, two accounts of Aesop's "golden goose" story are given in the book. In the first, the goose is killed out of rage because he wouldn't—or couldn't—lay more eggs for his owner. In the second, he's killed by the owner so as to remove whatever mechanism is inside him that creates the gold. On a surface reading, the first telling blames passion while the second blames reason. The real culprit, however, is ingratitude, which can as easily corrupt the head as the heart.

The goose-killers weren't grateful for the miracle of a golden egg laying goose—what an unlikely event! It's simply not natural for a goose to lay golden eggs, and it's simply not natural for man to live in the free, prosperous, peaceful society in which we find ourselves. No, we must not stagnate in the status quo, but neither must we take for granted the value of our free society. There has never been a better time to be alive —we've won the historical lottery, we should be grateful.

Another Form of Suicide

This brings me to my main problem with the book. Goldberg says on the first page that there is no God in his argument. He makes clear that he's not an atheist, but neither does his reasoning depend on the existence of a deity. In a sense, I appreciate what he's trying to do. He's making a limited case for Classical Liberalism and wants the opportunity to persuade people of that argument without being tangled up in more thorny metaphysical debates.

By and large, I think his description of the situation in which we find ourselves will be compelling to those who don't believe in a higher power. The historical, sociological, and psychological data backs up Goldberg's argument that we're prone toward tribalism and violence.

Yet, the prescriptive portion of the book, built as it is on the notion of gratitude, is unintelligible in a godless universe. Yes, it's good and right to be grateful for life, liberty, and the pursuit of happiness, but to whom are we grateful? Who receives our thanks? Does not gratitude imply a personal, transcendent "Other?"

Without such a being, our gratitude for the events of the past that brought us to the present becomes neutered into something like nostalgia. In Scripture, God's covenant people are often called to look back, but they do so with their feet in the present and their eye toward the future.

Looking to God's actions in the past will encourage and ennoble his people toward steadfastness and faithfulness in those things God is calling them to do in the moment and in the moments to come.

Nostalgia, on the other hand, is an indulgent retreat to yesteryear; leaving the real present for a glossy, sentimentalized version of a past that likely never was. Nostalgia is an existential form of suicide. Gratitude leads to good works, bravery, and life. If liberalism is the result of chance, nostalgia is the best we can hope for. If it's the result of divine providence, the gratitude for which Goldberg calls is not only possible, it's necessary.

Likewise, belief in God will keep us from being paralyzed with fear. It would be easy to walk away from Goldberg's book suspicious of any talk of "progress." But Christians live under the rule of a city that is to come. In Scripture, we find the words of that city's King, and in those words, we find the recipe for human flourishing in the here and now.

Thus we can amend and tweak the structures of the West responsibly, as happened with women's suffrage and the abolition of slavery. We look back with thanks, but we also march forward with hope.

The quote often attributed to Tocqueville is apropos, "America is great because America is good." Goldberg is surely correct in his claim that man's sinful nature is always ready to reappear. He's also right to suggest that the "Lockean Revolution" has birthed the freest, most prosperous civilization in history. He's wrong to think, however, that the free market and all that comes with it is enough to keep our nature at bay.

Our liberal democracy is dependent upon a virtuous citizenry, a virtuous citizenry is depended upon gratitude, and gratitude is dependent upon one to receive our thanks, a Giver of all gifts, a King above all kings. If the West is to be saved, she'll need a Savior.

33

AWAKENING THE WOKE: PERSUASION IN A TRIBAL AGE

T he identity politics practiced by liberals (i.e. social justice warriors) and conservatives (i.e. the alt-right) is soaking America in the acid of tribalism, leaving the fabric of our communal life threadbare. That's the gist of Noah Rothman's important new book, *Unjust: Social Justice and the Unmaking of America*. While he doesn't reference them, it struck me that his book is best understood as the final instalment of a trilogy, with the other two works being *The Coddling of the American Mind* by Greg Lukianoff and Jonathan Haidt and *Soul Searching: The Religious and Spiritual Lives of American Teenagers* by Christian Smith and Melina Lundquist Denton.

Rothman describes what he calls the "identitarian" politics of those whose university experience devalued rationality (Lukianoff and Haidt's thesis) and whose high school years over emphasized the emotive (Smith and Denton's thesis). If the books are read together, we can move from merely lamenting our politics to forming a proactive apologetic aimed at persuading those with whom we disagree.

Reducing the Rational

"Perhaps the simplest method for distinguishing classical liberals from militant social justice advocates" says Rothaman, "is the extent to which the latter are threatened by the articulation of challenging ideas." In order to understand the identity politics of the new right and left, one must understand the deep suspicion both groups have toward rationality. This is where *The Coddling of the American Mind* is helpful.

LUKIANOFF AND HAIDT make an argument that our educational system has isolated us from reason by coddling our safety, something that goes against the very essence of education. Say the authors:

> The notion that a university should protect all of its students from ideas that some of them find offensive is a repudiation of the legacy of Socrates, who described himself as the 'gadfly' of the Athenian people. He thought it was his job to sting, to disturb, to question, and thereby to provoke his fellow Athenians to think through their current beliefs, and change the ones they could not defend.

EDUCATION IS MEANT to make us uncomfortable, in other words. As teachers stopped pruning, prodding, and provoking, students sank more deeply into the cozy blankets of their already held beliefs.

Elevating the Emotive

If the rational is no longer preeminent, what is? Central to the answer given in *Soul Searching* is the notion of Moral Therapeutic Deism (MTD). In MTD, the chief end of man is to find happiness. "M" and "T" are easy to understand—God is something akin to a friendly therapist who wishes you'd be nicer. To understand the "D" part, it'll be helpful to say a word about classical deism circa the first half of the 19th century.

"Fix reason firmly in her seat," Thomas Jefferson insisted, "and call to her tribunal every fact, every opinion." Key to understanding classical deism is the revolutionary notion that reason, rather than scripture, is the benchmark of truth. Indeed, Jefferson went on to say that we should, "Question with boldness even the existence of a god; because, if there be one, he must more approve the homage of reason, than that of blindfolded fear."

The image Jefferson is evoking is that of a courtroom. When the bailiff says, "all rise!" the judge, "Reason," takes her seat. Pleading their case is every fact and opinion we might believe, waiting to be ruled acceptable or not by her honorable judge *Reason*. MTD is deistic in that it keeps the proverbial "self" as judge, but relocates the authority from the intellect to the emotive. We thus walk through reality as if we're Marie Kondo going through her closet, throwing away any and everything that doesn't spark joy—truth be dammed.

Persuasion in Our Tribal Age

With these two books in our minds, the grave story of identitarianism being told by Rothman becomes comprehendible: Our politics became tribal and instinctual as we devalued our rationality and idolized our emotions. To continue with the Jeffersonian illustration, is not the answer to impeach "her justice *Emotion*" and return "her honorable Judge *Reason*" to the bench? That's certainly the argument being made by many who often quote the famous Ben Shapiro quip, "facts don't care about your feelings." The implication is, your emotions are a terrible guide on the expedition of life. Which, to be fair, is true. However, is rationality the solution?

KEEP IN MIND, Jefferson didn't use his emotions to justify the holding of slaves—he rationalized it. Conversely, I don't think it was rationality that lead to the pro-choice backlash of Virginia Governor Ralph Northam's comments about post-birth abortion. Rationally, what makes the killing of a child ethical one minute (when it's inside the womb) but immoral the next (when it's outside the womb)? Even if infanticide is rationally defensible in light of pro-choice assumptions, it remains emotionally unbearable.

THE HOLDING of slaves and the killing of children are both wrong in God's world. Jefferson's rationality kept him estranged from reality when it came to slavery just as pro-choice advocates' emotions are keeping them tethered to reality when it comes to infanticide. Facts care neither about our feelings nor our rationality. Thus, by spending all of our energy commending reason and critiquing emotion we miss an opportunity to witness to the transforming power of the gospel, which takes away something and gives something to every cultural moment.

THE CHRISTIAN WORLDVIEW *takes away* our autonomy. Jackson's argument that reason should be the judge is the heart of all sin. It's not reason that's the problem, as we've said, it's the self. Jesus claims authority over our whole being. T.S. Elliot reminds us that we curtail this truth only to our own peril when it comes to evangelism:

> You will never attract the young by making Christianity easy; but a good many can be attracted by finding it difficult: difficult both to the disorderly mind and to the unruly passions.

THE CHRISTIAN WORLDVIEW takes control of our passion *and* our mind—taking away our ability to rationalize slavery, for example.

THE CHRISTIAN WORLDVIEW *gives* us justification. To those pro-choice advocates horrified by the thought of leaving a baby to die, we can offer a justification for that feeling—that baby is made in the image of God. If one is an atheist, there is a chasm between what "is" and what "ought" to be that their worldview can't rectify. The gospel offers a bridge to get one from "is" to "ought." It gives us a justification for our moral sentiments, a reason for our dogmatic intuitions that things are not as they should be.

ROTHMAN ENDS HIS BOOK SAYING, "No messiah will save us from ourselves... the hard work ahead falls on all of us." He's right to say it is ourselves from which we need saving, but that makes it even more odd that his solution to the problem is...ourselves. Indeed, our salvation will take nothing less than a messiah. Thankfully, such a savior has come and is coming.

ABOUT THE AUTHOR

Dustin Messer is a Senior Fellow at the Center for Cultural Leadership, leads the young adult and college ministry at All Saints Dallas, and teaches theology at Legacy Christian Academy in Frisco, TX. He also serves on the board of directors at both the Evangelical Fellowship in the Anglican Communion (EFAC-USA) and the Center for Christian Civics in Washington, DC. Before beginning his doctoral work at La Salle University, Dustin graduated from Boyce College and Covenant Theological Seminary, serving as Editor-in-Chief of Covenant's Bantam Journal during his time as a student. Having completed a fellowship at the National Review Institute, Dustin's writings have been published by many publications and organizations, including Christianity Today, Mockingbird, the Institute for Faith, Work, and Economics, the Alliance of Confessing Evangelicals, The Gospel Coalition, the Ethics and Religious Liberty Commission, Mere Orthodoxy, Dordt College's Center for the Advancement of Christian Education, and the Theopolis Institute.

ABOUT THE CENTER FOR CULTURAL LEADERSHIP

The Center for Cultural Leadership believes that culture should be Christian — not by political coercion, but by spiritual conversion. Christian is what Western culture was for 1000 years, and this what it should be today. This means that Christians should lead the culture — as fathers, mothers, college students, businessmen, attorneys, pastors, educators, software writers, salesmen, technicians, politicians, physicians, clerks, and so forth.

But CCL does not just believe Christians should lead. It shows them how to lead.

CCL is not only training Christian activists. Lots of people are doing that, and some are doing well. We're educating and equipping Christian transformationists. It's not enough to be active; you actually have to transform things. This is what we're after.

CCL is spearheading a new Christian culture by offering the following:

Fidelity: Biblical Faith in Family, Church and Culture, a hard-hitting, relevant, occasional journal written from a totally Christian perspective, and other incisive writings, too.

Institute for Cultural Leadership, conferences uniting leaders in fields as diverse as business, cinema, church, arts, economics and technology to strategize for greater effectiveness as cultural leaders.

CCL Publication Series and Kerygma Press: books, podcasts, monographs, booklets, and pamphlets, boldly pointing the way to a new Christian leadership in our society.

CCL website: christianculture.com, frequently updated and presenting news, editorials, and instruction from a distinctly Christian perspective, and showing ways to recapture our culture.

Marketplace Forums: local and regional meetings and conferences and seminars, training Christians to take the lead in culture, beginning right where God has placed them.

Annual national conference on cultural leadership, where relevant, knowledgeable, exciting speakers impart the truth of the as it relates to today's culture, and where you'll meet other Christians committed to taking their Faith seriously in modern life.

Center for Cultural Leadership
P. O. Box 100
Coulterville, CA 95041
831-420-7230
www.christianculture.com